Ancient Peoples and Places

THE ANGLO-SAXONS

General Editor

DR GLYN DANIEL

Ancient Peoples and Places

THE
ANGLO-
SAXONS

D. M. Wilson

79 PHOTOGRAPHS
37 LINE DRAWINGS
AND 1 MAP

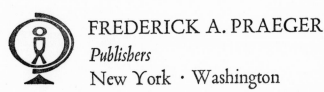

FREDERICK A. PRAEGER
Publishers
New York · Washington

THIS IS VOLUME SIXTEEN IN THE SERIES

Ancient Peoples and Places

GENERAL EDITOR: DR GLYN DANIEL

BOOKS THAT MATTER
Published in the United States of America in 1962
by Frederick A. Praeger, Inc., Publishers
111 Fourth Avenue, New York, N.Y. 10003
Second printing, 1962
Third printing, 1965
Fourth printing, 1967
© Thames and Hudson, London, 1960
All rights reserved
Library of Congress Catalog Card Number: 60–8369
Printed in Great Britain

C O N T E N T S

ILLUSTRATIONS

Foreword

THIS BOOK is intended to give a general view of Anglo-Saxon culture as seen through the eyes of the archaeologist. No book of this length can hope to do more than sketch the broad outlines of the subject; consequently I have had to be selective in my approach and I am only too conscious of the many gaps that occur in this story of six hundred years of the most formative period of English history.

It would be impossible to give separate acknowledgments for all the help I have received during the writing of this book, but I cannot allow it to go to press without some indication of my indebtedness. My thanks are due to Mr G. Ashburner for providing me with so many brilliant photographs. I am grateful to Professor Holger Arbman, Mrs S. Hawkes, Dr Ole Klindt-Jensen and Mrs M. Saunders for long hours of discussion of the problems of Anglo-Saxon archaeology. The day-to-day contact with my colleagues in the British Museum has provoked discussion, which has naturally influenced my thoughts on the subject, and my debt to them, and to the institution itself, cannot be sufficiently acknowledged. I would particularly like to thank Mr Julian Brown, who has allowed me to read, before publication, his revolutionary theories concerning the Lindisfarne Gospels, and Mr R. H. M. Dolley who, over a number of years, has patiently answered many questions on numismatic subjects. Mr Rupert Bruce-Mitford and Mr Peter Lasko kindly read the typescript of this book and offered me much advice and help which I deeply appreciate. I must thank the Early English Text Society for permission to use their translation of the riddle on p.122 and the editors of *Arms and Armour*, for the use of the translations of the passages of poetry on pp. 108 and 121.

Dr Daniel's encouragement and advice has helped me enormously and must be acknowledged here. I must thank my mother for her patience in reading through the typescript and putting in the commas. My wife has helped me immeasurably, with criticism, with typing and, above all, with her drawings – for she has drawn all but one of the line illustrations.

D.M.W.

INTRODUCTION: *The Study of*
Anglo~Saxon Archaeology

A T THE END OF THE nineteenth century archaeology had
emerged from the antiquarianism of the early Victorian
period, and from the quarrels attendant on the evolutionary
theories, into a rigid discipline based on two methods of study
– excavation and typology. General Pitt~Rivers had reduced
excavation to a science, carried out with military precision, and
had inculcated into the minds of the hitherto rather lackadaisical
field archaeologist a belief in scientific accuracy. It was many
years, however, before English archaeologists had learnt the
lessons he taught and reached the standard of thoroughness that
has placed English field archaeology in a position second to
none in the world. The second method of study was developed
in England by Sir John Evans and Pitt~Rivers, and in Scandi~
navia by Oscar Montelius and his disciple Bernhard Salin. A
close and detailed study of the material remains of ancient
peoples produced a system of 'typology'. The basis of typology
is the fact that manufactured objects are subject to evolutionary
processes. Sometimes the evolution can be seen as a gradual im~
provement in form or function, or both; occasionally it can only
be seen as a development in decoration. This is best illustrated
by Montelius's own example of the development of the railway
carriage. Starting as a horse~drawn coach, adapted to run on
rails, it developed in form through various stages: first as three
conjoined coaches made into one carriage until in the late
nineteenth century the only trace of its coaching ancestry was to
be seen in the curved bottoms of the side windows of the first~
class compartments. Typology can be used for its own sake or
applied chronologically. A typological sequence showing, say,
the development of the form of a particular type of brooch can

Fig. I

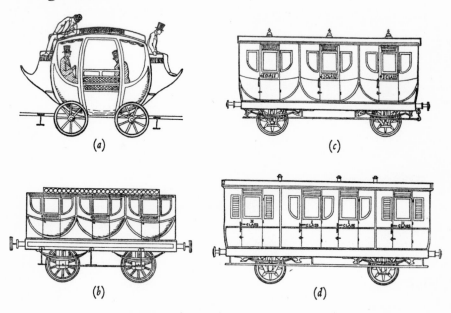

Fig. 1. Montelius's railway carriages: (a) England 1825; (b) Austria 1840; (c) and (d) Sweden/Germany c. 1850

then be used as a scale against which chronological judgments can be made. Thus an object found with a brooch of typologically early form might be said to be, in all probability, earlier in date than an object found with a brooch of the same group, but of a more developed form. The archaeologist calls this 'dating by association'.

The excavation, carried out between 1953 and 1957, by Mr Hope-Taylor of the site of a palace of an Anglo-Saxon king, at Yeavering in Northumberland, is only a brilliant extension of the methods used by General Pitt-Rivers on Cranborne Chase; the use of electrical and aerial methods of survey is nothing but a logical development in a sequence of technical improvements. Similarly Mr Leeds's study of the Anglo-Saxon square-headed brooches is an extension of the methods used by Oscar Montelius fifty-odd years ago.

Until the recent war there was a tendency for the archae-ologist to live in an ivory tower of his own devising; its founda-tions were excavation and cataloguing, and its superstructure new chronologies and typological judgments. In 1921, for in-stance, the late Dr Crawford defined archaeology as the study of 'the extra-corporeal limbs of man'; the study, in other words, of man's products, of his axes and spears, his houses and byres, his pots and pans. An arid subject indeed! But how much more arid was the doctrine of one of the greatest Anglo-Saxon archaeologists, Professor Baldwin-Brown, who, in 1915, wrote:

> The nature of the objects affects the archaeologist in so far as his knowledge of this enables him to group it with others of the same class, but his chief interest in it does not concern the probable conditions under which it was made and used, as much as its relationships to the other objects of its group.

This attitude was typical of that of many scholars and, apart from the very important social interpretations of the archae-ological material by Gordon Childe and the political perversions of the same material by the Nazis, archaeology remained bounded by the twin gods Oscar Montelius and General Pitt-Rivers. That it finally broke away from their constraining influence is due mainly to the genius of such teachers as Gordon Childe and Grahame Clark, who widened its scope beyond the narrow confines of the basic material, so that today the archaeological material is seen chiefly as the fossilized results of human behaviour. The modern archaeologist's aim is to try to reconstitute that behaviour without overtaxing his basic evidence.

This sketch of the recent history of archaeological technique is very necessary if we are to understand the archaeological methods that lie behind the study of the Anglo-Saxon period. Hodgkin in the preface to his *History of the Anglo-Saxons*, published in 1935, wrote, 'Saxon archaeology has not yet attained to a high degree of scientific security.' There can be no doubt that his statement was justified – but why?

When Hodgkin wrote those words there were perhaps four or five full-time Anglo-Saxon archaeologists working in England; none of them held teaching posts in the universities – they were all attached to museums. At the British Museum, Reginald Smith had ceased, some ten years earlier, to write on Anglo-Saxon subjects, although his enormous erudition was available to the scholarly world, while Sir Thomas Kendrick had just started his *Anglo-Saxon Art*. At the Ashmolean Museum Mr Leeds had just produced his book *Anglo-Saxon Art and Archaeology*, the first book on such a subject to be written since the publication of the British Museum's *Guide to Anglo-Saxon and Foreign Teutonic Antiquities* in 1923. Leeds's book was the published text of a series of lectures given at Edinburgh and, although full of interesting material, is, not unnaturally, badly balanced. At Cambridge Mr T. C. Lethbridge was excavating vast and complex Anglo-Saxon cemeteries. Today the position is a little better; there are perhaps a few more full-time Anglo-Saxon archaeologists in the country, but the only university teaching post in Anglo-Saxon archaeology is closely bound up with the teaching of Anglo-Saxon language and literature. Every student of Anglo-Saxon archaeology has, therefore, had to struggle, with little or no formal teaching, to a knowledge of the subject from other disciplines – English, History or Prehistory. Consequently it is hardly surprising that Anglo-Saxon archaeology – the Cinderella among antiquarian studies – is in a parlous state and, owing to the tremendous backlog of work, its methods often seem to be out of date to archaeologists of other periods and to historians, whose subjects have reached a stage of greater maturity. In order to answer

Hodgkin's criticism the Anglo-Saxon archaeologist must face up squarely to certain problems of his subject.

The student of the Anglo-Saxon period has the advantage of both archaeological and historical evidence in his study. That the two types of evidence can work admirably together is illustrated by the recent excavation of a royal township at Yeavering in Northumberland. There can be no doubt that this site, so ably excavated, is indeed *ad Gefrin*, the royal township mentioned by Bede as the place to which Paulinus went, with King Edwin, in 627 to preach Christianity to the people of Bernicia. The site will be discussed in greater detail in a later chapter, but it may not be out of place to mention here how, in the investigation of this site, archaeologists have helped historians and, conversely, how historians have helped archaeologists. The archaeologist provided for the historian, among other facts, some idea of the physical appearance of a Saxon royal township, the ground plan and probable reconstruction of the meeting place of a moot and a rough date for the abandonment of the site. The historian provided for the archaeologist the identity of the site, a knowledge of the likely purposes of the various buildings and a fixed date in a sequence of relative dates.

Such co-operation as this is not always quite so happy. There is a tendency for archaeologists to be tempted by the mirage of absolute historical dating. Rarely is the archaeologist so arrogant as to say, as one very great Anglo-Saxon archaeologist (E. T. Leeds) did say, '. . . for the early entries in the *Anglo-Saxon Chronicle* it is a question whether they are worth the vellum on which they were first written'; but too often the archaeologist jumps at a conclusion rather too hastily, just because it seems to fit an historical context. For instance, it has long been accepted by archaeologists, who based their belief on a detailed study of the contents of the graves, that there was considerable Frankish influence in Kent at the beginning of the sixth century. It seems probable that this influence was activated by the Franks follow-

ing their victory over the Visigoths at Vouillé in 507. Archaeologists have attempted to date the start of this influence on the
basis of the archaeological evidence. One scholar has recently
examined the problem in the light of a group of brooches: 'of
[Professor Kühn's] bow-brooch types of purely continental
origin, which are essentially radiate brooches, he [Kühn] finds
twenty specimens with localities in England, all in Kent except
two: seven (one Cambs, one Lincs) certainly made after 550,
one probably so, and one (Thuringian) of 525–575; and eleven
made before 550, three of which he dates 525–550 and eight
500–550, including two – the pair from Chatham Lines grave
2 – which he suggests were indeed made *c.* 500 or before 525,
but deposited rather after, since its contents as a whole belong
to Werner's Group II, 520–550. It is about 525, in fact, that
Kühn reckons the Frankish-Kentish relations thus displayed to
have begun. It seems, therefore, that the datings on which
Leeds suggested that in the time of Clovis, who died in 511,
Franks emigrated into Kent, cannot quite be held within that
line.'

In other words, largely on the basis of the two brooches from
Chatham Lines, which are dated by Professor Kühn to between 500 and 525, the date of the beginning of the Frankish
influence in Kent is moved forward by fourteen years.

There are 134 brooches, like those from Chatham Lines,
found in Europe, twenty-four of which occurred in association with other objects. One of these brooches was found in a
grave at Weimar with a copy of a coin of Zeno, the Byzantine
Emperor who reigned from 474–491; on this basis Kühn dates
the grave to between 500 and 550. But other brooches of this
group were found together with coins of Valentinian (364–75)
and of Anastasius (491–518), and one with a hoard of first-
century coins in a grave at Böckingen. The only statement that
can positively be made about this group is that the Weimar
burial must have taken place after 474. There is really no reason

– archaeological or historical – why all the brooches in this group should not have been made before 500; there is equally no reason why any of the brooches of this group should not have been placed in a grave at any period between, say, 475 and 575.

The fault of the author of this theory is that he has accepted *relative* dating as *absolute* dating. Kühn's dating system for these brooches, which is itself questionable, is a relative dating statement based on a chain of evidence which can best be illustrated by an adaptation of Montelius's formula: an object A found with an object B $(A+B)$ is dated with reference to a dated object E, through the link: $A+B=B+C=C+D=D+E$, each stage of the formula representing a different archaeological find. In such a case the margin of uncertainty must grow with every link until even relative dating statements are meaningless. This method of dating is too often used by Anglo-Saxon archaeologists, who, tempted by the accuracy of historical statements, try to date objects within limits that are too narrow. This is not to deny the value of typology and its concomitant, dating by association, in constructing a chronology. In prehistoric contexts the use of these methods is essential, for some sort of relative chronology must be built up as a working hypothesis. In the same way a similar structure is essential in the Anglo-Saxon period. But the use of this structure by an archaeologist in making fine historical judgments is completely indefensible.

It might be thought that, where a large number of objects are involved, dating by these methods might be more reliable. Dr Bertil Almgren, however, has recently shown statistically, by means of a study of the largest group of Viking brooches found in Scandinavia, that objects found in association with any individual brooch cannot be dated to within a century. The same reasoning is true of the whole of the pagan Saxon period. In the late Saxon period, however, it is possible to date certain objects, and particularly metalwork, more closely. First, a few

DATABLE LATE SAXON
ORNAMENTAL METALWORK

CENT.	PERSONAL DATING	OBJECTS ASSOCIATED WITH THE BURIALS OF HISTORICAL PERSONS	OBJECTS FOUND IN COIN HOARDS
7th		Certain objects from the coffin of St Cuthbert (*d.* 687)	Sutton Hoo (*c.* 650–60) Crondall (*c.* 670)
8th	The Tassilo Chalice (777–88) (made in Germany under strong English influence)		
9th	Alhstan's ring (817–67) K. Ethelwulf's ring (836–67) Q. Ethelswith's ring (855–89) Bp Ethilwald's seal (*c.* 850) The Alfred Jewel (871–99)		Sevington (*c.* 840–50) Hon, Norway (*c.* 855) Hexham (*c.* 850) Kirkoswald (*c.* 855) Beeston Tor (*c.* 871) Trewhiddle (*c.* 872–5) Talnotrie (*c.* 900)
10th			Cuerdale (*c.* 903–5)
11th		Pin of Abp Wolfstan of York (1002–1023) *King Edward the Confessor's Cross* (1042–66) *(lost)*	Igelösa, Sweden (*c.* 1006) Stockholm, Sweden (*c.* 1025) Sutton, Isle of Ely (*c.* 1066–87) *St Mary at Hill* (*c.* 1075) *(lost)*

objects can be dated because they are inscribed with the names of known historical figures; secondly, certain objects are found with coin hoards, which can now be dated with extreme accuracy; and, thirdly, certain objects are known to have belonged to certain historical people, having been found in their coffins, etc. The table opposite shows all the pieces of late Saxon ornamental metalwork found in such contexts.

It can be seen from this table that while there is a certain amount of dating evidence for the ninth and eleventh centuries, the evidence for the eighth and tenth centuries is practically non-existent. Even with these accurately dated parallels, few scholars would dare to date a piece of ornamental Saxon metalwork of this period to within a century, even with the help of the contemporary illuminated manuscripts. How very much more difficult to date the featureless axe or spearhead! More fragile objects can perhaps be more closely dated by coin evidence. It happens occasionally, as at Chester and Morley St Peter in Norfolk, that a hoard of coins is hidden in a pot. Such an object, because it is cheap and easily broken, may not have been of any great antiquity when it was buried, and the date of its manufacture can probably be placed within a few years of its deposition; but there are not many such pots. Precious objects, however, have a tendency to be handed down from one generation to another, as was the sword mentioned in 1015 in a will of the Atheling Athelstan: 'to my brother Edmund I grant the sword which belonged to King Offa'. The sword was more than two hundred and twenty years old when the prince died! On a humbler scale can be mentioned the case quoted by Mr Lethbridge of a ten-year-old girl, 'who was buried with brooches, girdle hangers and other things, which were worn or patched at the time of burial. She was provided with festoons of beads much too big for her. She was not buried with her own jewels, but with old and worn-out objects, which had probably belonged to her mother. They had been picked out of some old remnants chest. The cracked brooch with its missing garnets, the girdle hangers roughly patched for the occasion – these may have belonged once to her grandmother or great-aunt.'

This problem of absolute dating has exercised all who have written about Anglo-Saxon archaeology. Baldwin-Brown for instance, in the early years of this century, evolved a cypher by means of which he divided up each century into quarters, assigning archaeological material to one of these short periods. In the later years of his life, E. T. Leeds would often bend over backwards in an attempt to avoid too accurate a dating statement. In this book I must follow the example of Leeds: where a definite dating statement is made, it is made with all due qualifications; a book bristling with 'probably' and 'possibly' would make tedious reading: the reader must supply his own qualifications.

The Anglo-Saxon archaeologist must admit that his chronology is one of the weaker points in the present state of his subject's growth. Once this is admitted, a thorough study of the material can lead him to make historical judgments of a much broader type than those made by his predecessors. His material can be interpreted in its economic and social setting; he can make judgments about trade and about kingship, about diet and about craftmanship which were impossible fifty years ago. The time will come when a relative chronology can be erected for the whole of the Anglo-Saxon period on a basis acceptable to both the statistician and the historian. With the aid of new scientific methods, such as dendrochronology (tree-ring dating) and radio-carbon dating techniques, it may even be possible within the next fifty years to build up a reasonably accurate absolute chronology. We are not yet in this happy state, however, and, until we are, the Anglo-Saxon archaeologist must be wary of making historical judgments which have fine chronological implications.

To illustrate the way in which the Anglo-Saxon archae-ologist can help the economic historian, let us first take a statement made nearly twenty-five years ago by the greatest of all Anglo-Saxon historians, Sir Frank Stenton. 'The beginnings of English foreign trade', he wrote, 'lie in an obscurity which is only broken by occasional grants of freedom from toll to monasteries owning sea-going ships, by discoveries of early English coins on the Continent and by incidental references to trade or traders in ecclesiastical narratives.' Like others, archaeologists and historians, before him, he did not use the archaeological evidence, which tells of trading connections in luxury goods long before written evidence appears. European archaeology abounds in such evidence: Frankish glass, perhaps made on the Rhine, is found in Wales, Eastern Mediterranean pottery is found in Cornwall, and Byzantine silver in Suffolk. Rich silks from the East found in St Cuthbert's coffin are an indication of a considerable trade in such materials at an earlier period, while bronze bowls from Coptic Egypt, garnets from India and cowrie shells from tropical waters found in Anglo-Saxon graves tell of far-flung trading connections in the period before England had become Christian. In the later period Anglo-Saxon sword blade arse found in Norway and Anglo-Saxon coins occur in Polish hoards, while fragments of German stone mortars are found at Thetford. These material remains tell us as much of the direction and scope of the trade of Anglo-Saxon England as all the documents that the historian can produce. Mr G. C. Dunning, for example, in a lecture given in 1959, has traced, by means of the archaeological material, the changing currents of the cross-Channel wine trade, reinforcing historical evidence with material facts and filling in certain gaps in the historian's knowledge.

Such results as these are but a foretaste of things to come. In the future it is possible that the archaeologist will be able to help both the social and economic historian by excavating, completely, an Anglo-Saxon village. This has never been done – although recent excavations on the Continent, particularly those at Warendorf, enable us to gain some idea of the physical appearance and social organization of a contemporary German village. It is possible that the energetic work of the Deserted Medieval Village Research Group (which is engaged in indexing and surveying English villages that were deserted in the Middle Ages) will ultimately light on a village mentioned in Domesday, which has since been deserted, but which may provide in the hands of the excavator, some explanations of obscure points in that great Norman survey. The work already done by archaeologists is quite impressive; in recent years, palaces and water-mills have been excavated, defensive earth-works thoroughly investigated and discussed, and technical problems concerning the goldsmith's art and the blacksmith's products solved by practical experiment.

One particular branch of the study of the Anglo-Saxon period has developed by leaps and bounds in recent years. The investigations by such scholars as Mr Grierson, Mr Dolley and Mr Blunt of the problem of the Anglo-Saxon coinage have resolved many archaeological and historical problems. Problems of minting and moneying, of circulation and coinage reform have been answered, mainly by a re-examination of material already in collectors' trays. The body of numismatic evidence is so great that most new finds serve mainly to confirm the results of the re-examination of the material. For the first time, since the late nineteenth century, the problem of the decorative style of the Anglo-Saxon coinage has been tackled logically. For instance, Mr Dolley, in a thorough study of certain later coins of Aethelred II (979-1013), identified nine 'styles', each one distinguished by a different form of bust on the reverse of the coin. Each style is regional and has been given a geographical label – Northern, Southern, Eastern, etc. The historical implications of this have been followed up by Mr

Dolley who has suggested that the reason for the regional stylistic distinction at this stage of Aethelred's reign, where it had not occurred before, was a deliberate decentralization in the face of the great Danish attacks which culminated in Canute's conquest of the country. Such a conclusion can and does lead to other historical judgments which are of deep significance.

Numismatic judgments can similarly have great significance in relation to the archaeological material. For instance, Mr Grierson's study of the Merovingian coins found in the Sutton Hoo treasure not only enables historians to guess at the identity of the king commemorated by this burial, but enables archaeologists to construct some sort of chronology for the ornamental metalwork of the seventh century. Similarly Edgar's sexennial cycle of coin types, by which a new type of coin was issued every six years and the coins in circulation called in, has been recognized by the numismatist in the structure of the coin hoards of the tenth and eleventh centuries. The archaeological implications of the dating of hoards to within six years or less in the late Anglo-Saxon period are not yet fully appreciated.

From the work of the numismatist the Anglo-Saxon archaeologist can learn a lesson, for the methods of study are often very similar. The Anglo-Saxon archaeologist's material has been collected over a couple of centuries mainly from graves and hoards or found casually in isolation. It is common for a research student to take a group of these objects, the small-long brooches, for example, and study them, erect a typological structure based on his study, discuss its origin and degenerations and make a few remarks on its geographical distribution. All this is very valuable work and one of the great aims of the future Anglo-Saxon archaeologist must be to publish all the material lying neglected in museums up and down the country. But Anglo-Saxon archaeologists have never tackled certain problems which seem to me to be equally useful and interesting. Mr Jessup has discussed in detail the methods of manufacture of the Kentish garnet jewellery, but nobody has yet discussed the technical aspects of the structure of the Anglo-Saxon shield. Except in the cases of individual cemeteries, nobody has yet bothered to examine the skeletons found in Anglo-Saxon graves for evidence of longevity, disease or diet. Nobody has yet collected the evidence available in the Anglo-Saxon archae-ological material for carpentry, fishing, agriculture and similar pursuits. Many publications of Anglo-Saxon cemeteries contain short reports on the impressions of cloth rusted on the buckle plates or shield bosses, but nobody has yet gone round looking at every single example of impressed cloth structure on metal objects, although Mrs Crowfoot made a gallant beginning. Nobody in modern times has investigated thoroughly the interesting problems of dress and fashion in the period. All these are problems, typical of hundreds that could be listed, which could be worked on and discussed in the present stage of our knowledge.

By the detailed re-examination of the material remains, new facts are bound to emerge. The articles of Mr Jackson and Dr Fletcher on various aspects of Anglo-Saxon architecture demonstrate, most clearly, how such a re-examination can add to our appreciation of the period. Their recent re-appraisal of the Anglo-Saxon church at Lydd, for instance, has shown conclusively that this church must be one of the earliest in England and that it probably dates from the pre-Augustinian era. Their conclusions were reached by merely looking at the church in detail, with their minds completely free from pre-conceived ideas as to its structure.

Anglo-Saxon archaeology until the 1939–45 war was very largely a 'museum' study; the student examined objects in museums or excavated cemeteries, and then studied his finds in association with other objects in the same grave, and in relation to similar objects discovered elsewhere. Since the war, however, he has turned his attention much more to field work.

We have already mentioned the excavations at Yeavering carried out by Mr Hope-Taylor: to these can be added Group Captain Knocker's excavations on the site of the Anglo-Saxon town at Thetford, Sir Cyril Fox's classic study, based on work carried out before the war, of Offa's Dyke, the great linear earthwork which stretched along the border of Wales and Mercia, Mr Rutter's excavation of the Crossgates village site in Yorkshire, Miss Cramp's excavation of the site of Bede's monastery at Monkwearmouth and Mr Hope-Taylor's excavation of the royal manor at Old Windsor. These have initiated a programme of investigations of sites other than cemeteries which will continue to broaden our basic knowledge of Anglo-Saxon culture. What is more interesting is that the archaeologist has been working together with the historian on all these sites. In the words of Professor Grimes, 'The day is past when the historian, the philologist, the art historian and the archaeologist could ignore each other – not perhaps with impunity (for this was never so), but without attracting adverse criticism for such action. Today all four disciplines, and many others too, including the more purely scientific ones, must work together more closely if they are to make significant progress.'

In this book I have attempted to combine with the evidence of archaeology a measure, at least, of the evidence supplied by other disciplines, in an attempt to give an over-all picture of the material culture, the art and the social and economic status of our Anglo-Saxon forbears. This picture cannot be complete in a book of this length, and I can only hope that it will give a fair account, for the general reader, of the Anglo-Saxons as an organized society, seen through their material culture. The material culture of these peoples, as it survives today, is, as we shall see, of a very rich, but very limited, character. In the pagan period it is confined largely to the material found buried in graves. In the Christian period, when pagan burial practices to a large extent cease, the evidence rests largely on chance finds and such monumental remains as churches and stone crosses. Based on such sources, the picture I have painted is bound to be incomplete and in parts blurred, but it represents to the best of my ability the present state of our archaeological knowledge of the Anglo-Saxon period.

CHAPTER I

Historical Background
and Pagan Burials

To MANY the Anglo-Saxon period is seen as a no-man's-land, across which flit insubstantial, semi-legendary figures – Hengist and Horsa, Arthur, Alfred and Offa. The bleak outlines of the history of the period must be defined if we are to understand its archaeology.

It would be idle to expect to achieve a well-balanced view of Anglo-Saxon history in the course of the next few pages. Indeed, to the professional historian, the summary that follows may seem to contain merely a crude and uncritical appraisal of the period. This summary, as I have already said, is, however, intended for the non-specialist and not for the professional historian; the opinions it contains are based on those of the leading historians of the Anglo-Saxon period, to whose works the reader is referred in the bibliography.

The history of Anglo-Saxon England must be considered in three stages: (*a*) the pagan period from the settlement to the Augustinian mission, (*b*) the establishment of England, and (*c*) the Scandinavian era.

THE PAGAN ANGLO-SAXON PERIOD

No period of British history is so nebulous as the fifth century. Roman government, which had collapsed as the end result of a process of decline in the first few years of the fifth century, bequeathed a legacy of Roman institutions to Britain. The Romanized native population struggled for a short time to preserve its individuality and to retain its civilization, but was gradually submerged by inroads of invaders from the Continent.

'The newcomers,' wrote the Venerable Bede, '. . . came from three very powerful nations of the Germans, namely the Saxons, the Angles and the Jutes. From the stock of the Jutes are the people of Kent and the people of Wight, that is, the race which holds the Isle of Wight, and that which in the province of the West Saxons is to this day called the nation of the Jutes, situated opposite that same Isle of Wight. From the Saxons, that is, from the region that now is called that of the Old Saxons, came the East Saxons, the South Saxons and the West Saxons. Further, from the Angles, that is, from the country which is called *Angulus,* and which from that time until today is said to have remained deserted between the pro-vinces of the Jutes and Saxons, are sprung the East Angles, the Middle Angles, the Mercians, the whole race of the Northum-brians, that is, of those people who dwell north of the River Humber, and the other peoples of the Angles . . . In a short time, as bands of the aforesaid nations eagerly flocked into the island, the people of the newcomers began to increase so much that they became a source of terror to the very natives who had invited them.'

This passage, written nearly three hundred years after the events it describes, is unfortunately our best historical source for the origin of the English peoples. The accuracy and exact meaning of Bede's summary of the invasions has been argued *ad nauseam.* Ultimately our best course would seem to be to take it at its face value: the account is presumably based on legend and oral tradition, but Bede – a most careful and exact scholar – has apparently simplified a very complicated story.

First of all he mentions that the 'newcomers'– the Anglo-Saxons as we more conveniently call them – were *invited* to come to England by the native inhabitants. These invited peoples were known as *foederati,* mercenary soldiers brought to Britain towards the end of the Roman period to help defend the country against attack from Ireland, Scotland and the Continent; traces of their pottery, similar in form to that of their homeland, have been identified by Dr Myres at a number of

Roman military sites (Caister-on-Sea, Caister-by-Norwich, York, etc.). Secondly, Bede specifies the homelands of these *Fig. 2* people. The Saxons came from North Germany and Holland, from the area which was known in his day as Old Saxony, the Angles from the south of the Danish peninsula, from the area which is still called Angeln, and the Jutes from Jutland. In other words, the Anglo-Saxons came from the western coast-lands of Europe, from the area between the mouth of the Rhine and central Jutland. Their invasions must be seen against the background of similar tribal movements throughout Europe, movements which are so important that the contemporary period on the Continent is designated 'the Migration period'.

A sixth-century Byzantine writer, Procopius, divides the invaders of Britain into two, Angles and Frisians, and there is probably a kernel of truth in his statement. Although the Frisians apparently inhabited the coastlands of North Holland, it is possible that at this time the Frisians and Saxons had merged into one people, the Frisians losing their identity in the process, a not uncommon occurrence in the Migration period. In fact, by the time that the English settlement had got under way it is probable that all these peoples, Angles, Saxons and Frisians, and to a lesser extent the more independent Jutes, had become more or less identified with each other, an opinion which is to a certain extent supported by the mixed character and origin of the earliest Anglo-Saxon grave-goods. The Anglo-Saxon peoples, then, were probably of mixed stock, with a number of common characteristics, before they arrived in England.

The invaders came in bands, headed by aristocratic leaders, to settle in a new land, at first in small groups, later combining into larger units. The date of the most important incursions of the Anglo-Saxons took place, Myres has argued, 'within ten years of the middle of the fifth century'. Our knowledge of the course of the invasions is based on both archaeological and historical sources – neither of them very secure. They came both in the guise of colonists and as mercenaries.

That the Roman policy of employing mercenaries was continued in the post-Roman period is well illustrated by the history of the semi-legendary Vortigern and Hengist and Horsa. Vortigern, 'a proud tyrant', employed Teutonic mercenaries under two leaders, Hengist and Horsa, to help him repel the Picts and the Scots. The colony, founded by Vortigern in the east of England, must have been strengthened by accretion from the Continent, until the mercenaries rebelled against their employers and started to colonize the country in earnest. The names of these people may be legendary but it is reasonable to suppose that parts of England – Kent and Sussex for instance – were settled in this manner. The conquest of the rest of England probably started, as did the colonization of America, with small bands camping on the eastern seaboard and gradually spreading west up the river valleys into the rest of the country. The Britons, under such legendary heroes as Arthur, for example, put up a considerable resistance against the Saxons. Gradually, however, over a period of some hundred and fifty years they were reduced to the position of a subject population, or fled to the hills and fastnesses of the Celtic lands to the west and north. At the time of the Augustinian mission the Anglo-Saxons controlled the whole of England from Kent to East Dorset and from the East Coast to the lower Severn, Staffordshire and Derbyshire, most of Yorkshire and part of Northumberland and Durham. The conquest of Britain continued sporadically for many years – the Edwardian wars of the Middle Ages are but the logical conclusions of an expansion that was continuous from the middle of the fifth century.

THE ESTABLISHMENT OF ENGLAND

The presence of a large number of tribal leaders in the early years of the settlement resulted in the establishment in England

Fig. 2. Kingdoms and peoples of Anglo-Saxon England. Inset: the Continental homeland of the Anglo-Saxons. (Scale approx. ½ main map)

of numerous royal dynasties. The relations between these dynasties was more often bloody than friendly, but there is good
reason to believe that the new settlers regarded themselves more
as Anglo-Saxons than as members of their own particular
Kingdom. The late sixth and seventh centuries are often
lumped together by historians under the heading 'the period of
the heptarchy'. There were, however, more than the seven
kingdoms implied in this title existing at one period or another.
These were Northumbria (occasionally divided into two kingdoms – Bernicia, between the Tees and the Forth, and Deira,
between the Humber and the Tees), Lindsey (roughly Lincolnshire and East Anglia), Mercia (roughly the present-day
Midlands), Essex, Middlesex, Kent, Wessex and Sussex,
which were all at one time or another kingdoms, with kings
who traced their ancestry from Woden or from another
Germanic god, Seaxneat. The history of the period from 600 to
the Conquest tells of the gradual movement of the main centre
of power from north to south, from Northumbria to Wessex.
It is also the story of the reduction of the power of these kingdoms and their ultimate unification under one man.

One of the most important influences of the period was, of
course, that provided by the church. The mission of St
Augustine, which started in 596, and the consequent conversion of the country, were to bring literacy to the Anglo-Saxons
and organization to the central government; but, as Sir Frank
Stenton has pointed out, the church was more a hindrance than
a help to the unity of the country. The establishment of the
Archbishopric of York in 734, for example, split the ecclesiastical and, to some extent, the secular government of the country
into two. Northumbria was throughout the middle period of
Anglo-Saxon history regarded as a distinctly separate part of
the country; as witness, for instance, King Alfred's use of the
terms 'on this side of the Humber' and 'beyond the Humber' in
the introduction to his translation of Gregory's *Cura Pastoralis*.

In the early days of Anglo-Saxon Christianity, Northumbria was the most important kingdom in England. In the seventh century the Northumbrian kings, Edwin, Oswald and Oswiu, came within an ace of establishing a permanent overlordship over the whole of England. But in 658 this hope of unity was ended by the revolt of the Mercians, when Wulfhere took the throne of Mercia. Although we have a clear picture of the kings of Northumbria from the hand of Bede, himself a Northumbrian, the northern kingdom never again achieved the power it had under Edwin and Oswald.

Meanwhile Mercia had absorbed the kingdoms of Essex and East Anglia (with Lindsey), the rulers of these two areas becoming subject to their Mercian overlord. By about 670, London, the great mercantile centre of England, had come under their control. During Wulfhere's reign Wessex became subject to Mercia, as did Sussex and the Isle of Wight. Wulfhere was defeated by the Northumbrians at the end of his reign and his successor, Aethelbald, was left to complete the task of building up Mercian supremacy over the whole of England. It was Aethelbald's cousin Offa (757–796) who was to be the strongest Mercian king, *rex totius Anglorum patriae* (King of the whole of England) as he described himself in one of his charters. In 796 Cenwulf succeeded Offa and until 821, when he died, Mercian supremacy remained firm and established. Over a number of years following Cenwulf's death, however, Egbert, king of Wessex, after a series of campaigns in Mercian territory received the submission of all the lands formerly ruled by Offa. From now on, the fortunes of the royal house of Wessex were to control the Anglo-Saxon kingdom.

THE SCANDINAVIAN ERA

In 793 the Viking raiders descended on England and Western Europe:

'In this year,' says the *Anglo-Saxon Chronicle,* 'dire portents appeared over Northumbria and sorely frightened the people. They consisted of immense whirlwinds and flashes of lightning, and fiery dragons were seen flying in the air. A great famine immediately followed those signs, and a little after that in the same year, on 8th June, the ravages of heathen men miserably destroyed God's church on Lindisfarne, with plunder and slaughter.'

They came to a land, rich and comparatively peaceful, to plunder, pillage, rob and rape. England was a home of learning, the centre of a prosperous merchant and agricultural community, and was completely unprepared for the sudden menace from the Scandinavian lands of the misty North. At first the invaders came in small bands merely to plunder, but, by the middle of the ninth century, great organized armies were ravaging the countryside. Mercia and Northumbria were conquered by the invaders and Wessex was sore pressed. Alfred's defeat of the Viking marauders at Edington in 878 called a halt to a series of Viking victories which had brought much of England under the control of the Scandinavians. From 878 and onwards, under Alfred and his successors, the Viking raiders, who had now settled in the north and east of England, were gradually brought under the control of the English crown.

Traditionally these early Vikings are known as Danes, although doubtless by the time they were settled in England they were a people of mixed Scandinavian blood. In the early years of the tenth century Lancashire and Cheshire, and the north-west generally, were invaded from Ireland by a group of Norwegian Vikings and the internecine wars between the two elements, Danish and Norwegian, considerably aided the conquest of Northumbria by the Mercians and the West Saxons under Edward the Elder and Aethelstan, who has been described as the most brilliant of English kings. Not only did Aethelstan conquer the north and establish friendly relations with its aristocracy, but he also conquered Cornwall and became one of the elder statesmen of Europe, consulted by the Emperor, the Normans and the Scandinavians. He estab-lished a sound civil service and reformed the coinage. From the death of Aethelstan in 939 there is a marked decline in the strength and prestige of the English kings. Wars with Viking raiders and bad counsel at home depleted the strength of the kingdom and only under Edgar (959–975) was any of the former brilliancy of English government achieved. Edgar's greatest achievements were in the field of artistic patronage and in the monastic revival that took place under the great Church-men, Oswald, Aethelwold and Dunstan – the latter credited by one chronicler with 'holy guile'.

In the years following Edgar's death the Viking attacks were renewed and, although these were resisted with spirit and some success, the conquest of England by Sweyn and Canute in the early years of the eleventh century was a foregone conclusion. Canute came to the throne of England in 1016 and for nine-teen years governed from England an Empire which, in name at least, extended from the shores of the Baltic to the Isles of Scilly. The great Anglo-Scandinavian Empire could only be controlled by an immensely strong king and collapsed in 1042 on the death of Harthacnut, the son of Canute. The English dynasty of Wessex regained the throne in the person of Edward the Confessor, who had grown up at the court of the Dukes of Normandy. During his reign Norman influence in England increased, the church, the law and the administration being influenced by contemporary French institutions. These Nor-man elements in pre-Conquest England were, to a certain extent, counteracted by the rude Anglo-Saxon nationalism of William's distant cousin, Harold. When, on the death of Edward and the succession of Harold, William, Duke of Normandy, claimed the English throne, England was to some extent prepared for Norman government. Much that was good in Anglo-Saxon England survived the Norman Conquest, which centralized the government of the country and unified England once and for all.

PAGAN ANGLO-SAXON ARCHAEOLOGY

It is a commonplace that the pagan Anglo-Saxon archae-ology of this country can only be studied from the material deposited in the graves of the newly arrived population, from their brooches, buckles, weapons and pottery. Much of this material will be treated in greater detail under separate headings in later chapters of this book. Here I wish to discuss the im-plications of this material in a broader context.

The Anglo-Saxon peoples practised both inhumation and cremation in the burial of their dead. The two rites take many forms. Although most Anglo-Saxon inhumations were in an extended position, crouched burials, in which the body has been buried with the knees beneath the chin, are by no means unknown. Other variations also occur. At Abingdon, for example, one skeleton lay on its face with the left arm raised and bent across the forehead. Sometimes a double burial is found, where the body has been placed in an old grave with the under-lying body disturbed and disarticulated; occasionally two bodies were buried side by side. Cremation also can take various forms, though usually the burnt bones were collected and placed in an urn. A traveller at the court of King Alfred tells how in the Baltic lands there was a custom 'that in every tribe the dead shall be burned, and if a single unburned bone is found, great atonement shall be made for it.' Care of such a quality is reflected in many of the cremation cemeteries of England, but occasionally the cremation was not so complete. Both inhumation and cremation burials occur in flat cemeteries and in barrows and mounds. The occurrence of mixed in-humation/cremation cemeteries is frequently recorded, even in the West Saxon area, where the ritual was more usually inhumation – out of 201 graves excavated at Abingdon, for example, only 82 were cremations. There seems to be little chronological implication in either form of burial: cremations occur both early and late in the pagan Anglo-Saxon period and the same is true of inhumations. It is often stated that cremation was a feature of the early Anglo-Saxon period, having been gradually replaced later by the use of inhumation, and that in mixed inhumation/cremation cemeteries the crema-tions are the earlier burials. There may be an element of truth in this (especially in the Thames Valley) but, as Mr Leth-bridge has pointed out, at Lackford in Suffolk, 'cremation survived . . . to the end of paganism', and the occurrence of a late form of square-headed brooch at Abingdon in a crema-tion burial shows that Mr Lethbridge's statement is true of the West Saxon region as well.

The Saxons tended not to use old Romano-British cemetery sites. The sites of Hassocks and Ringmer in Sussex, which are often quoted in an attempt to support this continuity, are apparently accidental re-usages of an ancient site. The Roman pottery from Hassocks, for example, cannot be dated much after the middle of the third century. The considerable Anglo-Saxon cremation cemetery on the Mount of York, however, was right in the middle of the Roman city's principal burial place and this, at least, does demonstrate a continuity between Roman and Anglo-Saxon cemetery usage. But such cases are rare and we have little evidence which would enable us to relate the Anglo-Saxon burials to their Roman counterparts.

The Anglo-Saxon dead were buried with their most intimate personal possessions, brooches, work-box and chate-laine in the case of a woman, spear, shield and sword in the case of a man. Occasionally they were buried with food (at Melbourn a sheep's jaw was found in the grave, while at another Cambridgeshire cemetery eggs were found in an urn) and drink, which was held in the smaller, secondary pottery vessels found in inhumation cemeteries. In cremation burials personal possessions were often burnt with the body; if not, they were often represented by small, unburnt model combs, knives, etc., placed in the urn with the ashes. Features such as the food and the model tools suggest that this is something more than the habit found in a number of modern societies of dressing-up a corpse in its best clothes. The body was being sent off into the after-life with the belongings it would need there, some men even being placed in their ship, as at Snape. As the surviving vernacular literature was written by Christians – usually by priests – it is hardly surprising that there is in this country little written evidence concerning pagan burial practices. We have to turn to the evidence provided by the Scandinavian literature for information concerning such burial rites. The following passage from *Ynglinga Saga* is typical of many passages which could be quoted here:

'The burning was carried out in a splendid manner. At that time it was believed that the higher the smoke rose in the air, the loftier would be the position of the burnt man in heaven; and the more possessions that were buried with him the richer he would be.'

The great Anglo-Saxon epic poem *Beowulf* yields some evidence regarding the practices of pagan burial. Consider, for example, the burial of Beowulf himself:

'Then the people of the Geats, as he had asked them, constructed a splendid pyre on the ground, hung with helmets, war shields and shining corselets, in the midst of which the lamenting warriors laid the glorious prince, their beloved lord. Then the warriors began to light the greatest of funeral pyres on the hill, the wood smoke rose high, black above the fire; the roaring flame mingled with the weeping (the tumult of the wind ceased) until it had consumed the body hot to its heart ... The people of the Wedra then raised a high, broad barrow on the cliff; it could be seen from afar by seafarers; in ten days they built the beacon of the bold warrior. They surrounded the remains of the pyre with a wall, constructed as worthily as skilled men could do. They laid rings and jewels in the barrow.'

The passage then tails off into semi-Christian sentiment, but the pagan elements are plain. Among other funerals recorded in *Beowulf* is one in which a ship is loaded with the body and treasure, and pushed out to sea.

The idea of a journey to the world of the dead is almost as universal as is the idea of furnishing the body with weapons, tools, ornaments and food. It would be tedious to labour the point. However, it is as a result of the Anglo-Saxons' belief in this idea that we have the large quantity of pagan Saxon material in our museums today.

THE ARCHAEOLOGY OF

THE ANGLO-SAXON SETTLEMENT

From 1913 until his death in 1955, E. T. Leeds, in a series of books and articles, attempted, on the basis of a minute study of the archaeological material, to define the areas of the Anglian, Saxon and Jutish settlement. This was mainly based on a typological study of the humbler type of Anglo-Saxon brooch. One of his most important observations, however, is based on a geographical fact: Anglo-Saxon cemeteries, he noted, bore no distributional relationship to the Roman road system; the newcomers advanced into, and settled, the country along the river valleys. He further pointed out that the Anglo-Saxons also avoided the Roman towns and forts, the great deserted stone buildings of the Romans which were described in the literature as 'cunning work of giants'. We have already noted that continuity in the use of cemeteries between the Roman and Anglo-Saxon periods is a rare occurrence. This lack of interest on the part of the Saxons in the social machinery of Roman Britain – in its daily life, its communications, its villa system, its organized army and its central government – is an interesting and unexplained feature of their settlement.

Leeds's picture of this *horror romani* needs perhaps a little quali-
fication today. Mr S. Frere's recent excavations have shown
that there was a Saxon settlement of an extremely early period
within the Roman town at Canterbury and there were certainly two early cremation cemeteries of some size at York.
Again, it is clear that in north and east Kent, at any rate, the
Anglo-Saxon cemeteries are closely related in their distribution
to the Roman roads.

Leeds's attempt to distinguish the Anglian, Saxon and
Jutish elements in the burial material met with varying success.
We have seen how the national character of the newcomers at
the time of the invasions was already very mixed: this mixture
is reflected in the archaeological material. Certain features of
the Saxon element among the invaders, however, are clearly
distinguishable. The distribution of early saucer brooches, for
example, as studied by Mr Leeds and more recently by Mrs
Saunders, shows a concentration in south-east England and
the Thames Valley – an area traditionally designated Saxon.
Such saucer brooches have their origin on the lower Rhine, in
the area of the Saxon homeland. Similarly a group of small
square-headed brooches, of an early date, found in Kent and
paralleled to some extent in the Danish material, help to vindi-
cate Bede's statement as to the Jutish origin of the Kentish
people. Dr Myres suggested that a study of the pottery would
seem to indicate that East Anglia received more direct im-
migration from Schleswig than did Northumbria, which, as
Mr Hunter Blair has pointed out, came under Saxon rule as
much as a result of the revolt of Saxon mercenaries employed by
the Romano-Britons, as by direct colonization. But generally
speaking the archaeological material of the period of settlement
is so mixed that attempts to distinguish it tribally are vain.

We must not forget that there were Anglo-Saxon mercenaries in Britain before the Roman abandonment of the province. The mercenaries took over the districts which were too

weak to oppose them and invited their cousins from across the North Sea to come and share their spoils. The mercenaries were presumably of very mixed origin, as were their cousins, and they combined to contribute to the muddle that comprises the archaeological record, a muddle in which, in a single cemetery, older Romano-Saxon pottery occurs alongside both Anglian and Saxon pottery and in which Saxon brooches occur in both Anglian, Saxon and Jutish areas.

Broadly speaking, however, once the preliminary muddle of the invasion period was over, and once the newcomers had become established, certain features in the archaeological material clearly distinguish the Essex–Wessex–Sussex area from the Yorkshire–Mercia–Suffolk area and both of these from the rich Kentish area. How much of this material is tribal in the sense of 'Anglian', 'Saxon' or 'Jutish', and how much is regional, is a problem that must now be examined.

One of the chief archaeological features of Anglo-Saxon Kent is the garnet-ornamented jewellery – for although some of this jewellery occurs elsewhere, it has long been obvious that it is mainly concentrated within that county. The discovery, however, of a large quantity of garnet jewellery at Sutton Hoo in Suffolk encourages the archaeologist to reconsider his previously held views. For the Sutton Hoo jewellery, while related in certain technical features to the Kentish material, has also many unique features. The differences are sufficient to enable us to recognize a distinct Kentish culture, at once individual and wealthy, which must be based almost completely on economic circumstance and not on tribal differences. Kent's geographical position and its rich soils have always made it a wealthy county. Most scholars nowadays would agree that this garnet jewellery flourished in the last half of the sixth century and in the first half of the seventh, and that it reflects the richness and importance of the settled area, an importance which can be seen, for example, in the historical figure of King

43

Aethelbert of Kent who had strong Continental connections. But to call this jewellery 'Jutish', as is so often done, is to miss the whole significance of the Kentish problem. Dr Hodgkin was on the verge of solving the problem when he said, 'The Jutish nation . . . was made after the Conquest. It was to all intents made in Kent.' In fact the historians have been using the word 'Jutish' when they meant 'Kentish'. Bede's *'Jutarum natio'* in Kent and the Isle of Wight has been torn from its context; it means surely that the earliest settlers in those areas were organized under leaders from Jutland and received reinforcements from that area as well as from other northern European areas. It follows that once the newcomers had become established in the Kentish area they would, under the influence of their new environment and of their geographical situation in relation to the Franks, develop a material culture of their own, just as they developed a legal system and a nation of their own.

Our picture of the material culture of the Angles and the Saxons is not quite so well defined. The archaeological evidence within the areas occupied by these peoples rests largely on a study of their jewellery, the Anglo-Saxon equivalent of the mass-produced jewellery sold today in the cheaper chain stores. The distribution of this material, when divided typologically, falls into two groups which can be classed as Anglian and Saxon. For instance, as we have seen, one of the leading Saxon types of brooch is the saucer brooch, which has a distributional concentration in the Upper Thames Valley, Sussex and Berkshire, with a number of outliers in the southern Midlands. This type of brooch is reasonably common in the continental Saxon homeland and its Saxon distribution in England is quite convincing. Similarly the small group of wrist clasps appear to be typically Anglian, if judged only by their geographical distribution. I believe, however, that we must be rather more careful in attaching these tribal names to objects just because they are found in the broad area in question.

The distribution of a certain type of cruciform brooch (Åberg III and IV) is clearly centred on the Cambridge region, with outliers in Yorkshire and Mercia. So far, admittedly, not a single brooch of this sort has been found in the Saxon region, yet the type can hardly be considered as typical of the whole Anglian area. Rather, it is a fashion that grew up in a smallish area and which was then traded out of that area into other districts. Other so-called Anglian types occur over such a wide area that although they were presumably made in one particular district, it is impossible to distinguish them by any other title than 'Anglian'.

The wide distribution of objects resulting from trade must always be borne in mind. We shall revert to this subject in a later chapter, but a few examples may be quoted here to demonstrate the mobility of objects at this early stage of Anglo-Saxon history. Anglo-Saxon jewellery has been found in Germany, pottery from the Low Countries carried wine to Kent, and chatelaine rings of African ivory are of reasonably common occurrence in Anglo-Saxon graves, while cowrie shells came from the tropical waters of the Indian Ocean. When we know that objects such as these travelled thousands of miles to local markets we cannot rely too closely on a scattered distribution of a handful of cheap brooches over the whole face of England.

SUTTON HOO

Space prohibits a full discussion of the thousands of Anglo-Saxon graves found in England, but one of these graves, found at Sutton Hoo near Woodbridge in Suffolk, deserves consideration at some length. The grave produced the richest and most brilliant treasure ever found on British soil; it is, indeed, only paralleled in Europe by the funerary treasure of Childeric, King of the Franks who died in 481. Childeric's treasure was found at Tournai in Belgium in 1653, but only a few fragments survived the robbery at the Cabinet des Medailles in Paris in

1831. Many rich graves had been found in England before the discovery of Sutton Hoo – Taplow in Buckinghamshire, Broomfield in Essex, Cowlow in Derbyshire and a whole host of graves in Kent – but all pale into insignificance by the side of this East Anglian king's treasure.

The excavators of Sutton Hoo in 1939 came to an oval mound with a central hollow, lying on the edge of an escarp-ment overlooking the river Deben. The shape of the mound was eventually explained by the fact that a ship had been buried in it; the hollow in the middle proved to have been caused partly by the collapse of a wooden mortuary chamber amidships and partly by the attentions of some sixteenth- or seventeenth-century antiquarians, who had tried to rob the grave by sinking a shaft in the centre of the mound. All that remained of the ship were the marks in the sand of the decayed wood, marks which were skilfully isolated by the excavators so that a plan or the ship and photographs of it in its entirety could be made. The original over-all length of the ship must have been about eighty-six feet, of which some eighty feet were traced. It was a clinker-built ship of a type paralleled by the ship found at Nydam in South Jutland. Unlike the well-known Viking ships, it was a rowing-boat; there was no seating for a mast and traces of a rowlock survived on the port gunwale. No seats or decking were found but in the centre were traces of the gabled mortuary chamber which contained the burial deposit.

Fig. 17

No body was found in the ship – no traces of human bones. The burial must, then, be considered as a cenotaph, a monu-ment to a great man: the treasure and paraphernalia found in the grave leave no doubt that this was the memorial of a king.

The objects found in the burial chamber can be divided into three groups: (a) domestic utensils and minor weapons, (b) personal ornaments and personal weapons, and (c) royal regalia. The objects classed under the first heading include a quantity of chainwork, iron-bound wooden buckets, cauldrons,

a pottery bottle (which in form resembles the wheel-
turned pottery of Kent), a group of spears and angons (see
below, p. 123), an iron-hafted battle-axe and a number of iron
objects of indeterminate use. The remains of a musical instru-
ment, which has been reconstructed as a rectangular harp,
was taken to pieces before burial and placed inside a cast
bronze bowl, which had been imported from Alexandria.
Also found were the remains of a set of silver-mounted drinking-horns and gourds. One of the largest horns has been reconstructed and found to have a capacity of some six quarts
and must have come from the head of the now extinct aurochs.
All these objects are paralleled in other Anglo-Saxon contexts, with the exception of the iron-hafted axe. Other objects,
however, must be classed in this group, some of which are
rather more exotic – the great circular silver dish of Byzantine
origin which bears the control stamps of the Emperor Anastasius (491–518), for example. Other pieces of Mediterranean
silver plate include a large fluted silver bowl, which was found
underneath the large dish; it bears in a central, circular field a
late classical female head in low relief. A silver ladle and a
small cup were found, together with a set of ten hemispherical   Plate 3
silver bowls. In the centre of each bowl was inscribed a simple
geometrical or semi-floral design. Two very significant pieces
are a pair of spoons of a well-known classical type, which bear
the names Saul and Paul in Greek characters. This allusion to
the conversion of the Apostle must symbolize the conversion or
the baptism of an important person.

Finally, we must class in this group a series of three bronze
bowls fitted with loops for suspension and ornamented with
circular, and, in one case, with square as well as circular,
panels of enamelled ornament. These belong to a large and
common group of antiquities, known as 'hanging-bowls',
which continued to be made until well on into the eighth
century, some late variants being found in Viking Age graves

in Scandinavia. The decoration of the applied enamelled panels is Celtic rather than Anglo-Saxon in origin; it is most commonly based on developed spiral motifs, sometimes, as at Sutton Hoo, being further decorated with small pieces of mille-fiori glass floated into the enamel. These millefiori fragments are cut from a rod made up of many stretched and twisted strands of different coloured glass, in the fashion of the multi-coloured 'rock' popularly sold at seaside resorts. There has been a con-siderable amount of discussion concerning the purpose and origin of these bowls. The presence of a model fish, standing on a column in the centre of the Sutton Hoo bowl, and the fact that many of the bowls have an escutcheon on the inside, suggest that they held some clear liquid; the suggestion has recently been made that they were used as a kind of ecclesiasti-cal 'finger-bowl', although there is still a certain amount of support for the theory that they were used as sanctuary lamps. The fish in the Sutton Hoo hanging-bowl may be the well-known Christian symbol; if so, a liturgical use is not ruled out. On the other hand, if the bowl held water, the fish would then be in its natural element and its use here might merely be the craftsman's conceit. These bowls were apparently made in a Celtic area, presumably in Northumbria: Dr Françoise Henry's contention that they were made in Ireland is not entirely convincing in the face of their rarity in that country and their ubiquity in the Anglo-Saxon area.

Plate 11

The second group of objects in the Sutton Hoo cenotaph comprises the personal equipment which was laid out along the line of the keel, in the centre of the mortuary chamber. It forms by far the most exciting group of objects in the grave. The three major weapons, the sword with its jewelled pommel and scabbard, the shield with its bird and dragon figures, and the helmet, covered with plates of impressed ornament, are closely paralleled in the rich graves of Uppland in Sweden and, al-though no really convincing case has yet been made out for the

Plate 2

Plate 8

actual physical importation of these objects from Sweden, the probability is strong enough to deserve serious consideration. All the personal ornaments, however, are certainly of English manufacture and are remarkable as much for their richness as their quantity. Other than the mounts of the sword, nineteen pieces of gold jewellery were found in the grave, the largest and most impressive of which is the great gold buckle, which is 5·2 Plate 7 inches long and weighs over fourteen ounces. The front face of this object is covered with most skilfully interlaced, asymmetrical snakes, bordered by interlaced, elongated animals. The loop ot the buckle has a slightly more regular, plain ribbon interlace, but the circular plate, behind the tongue, has more interlaced snakes. All the ribbon-like bands on the buckle plate and on the circular tongue plate are decorated with incised circles within bordering lines, all inlaid with niello. Three great plain dome-headed rivets connect with sliding catches on the hinged back plate.

There is a striking difference between the great gold buckle and the more flamboyant, polychrome jewellery, which makes up the greater part of the personal ornaments. The purse-lid, Plate 9 for example, consisted of a border, made up of twisted wire filigree, and panels inlaid with garnet and coloured glass which enclosed a piece of ivory, leather or other material, in which were set seven plaques and four studs. The plaques and studs are inlaid with garnets and mosaic glass: in the top centre is a plaque containing four animals, set in pairs, whose limbs interlace; this is flanked by two hexagonal mosaic plaques. Below each of these is a plaque portraying a man between two rampant beasts, while in the centre bottom of the purse are two affronted plaques showing small, duck-like birds caught in the claws of birds of prey. The height of perfection in this poly-chrome technique is reached in the pair of curved clasps that Plate 1 hinge centrally on a gold, animal-headed pin. The clasps were sewn to their cloth or leather base through a series of strong

Fig. 3

lugs. Each half of each clasp is, in all major respects, similar to the others, although there are slight variations in each piece. The curved end takes the form of two boars, so interlocked that their hindquarters form the outer element of the ornament, their heads appearing in the centre. In the spaces between the heads and feet are panels of delicate filigree animal ornament.

Fig. 3. Interlocked boars from the Sutton Hoo clasps

The rest of the plaque consists of a rectangular frame, ornamented with a series of interlaced, ribbonlike creatures, which encloses a carpet pattern of polychrome cellwork. In no other piece of jewellery from Sutton Hoo does the quality of workmanship surpass that demonstrated by the clasps. The garnets are cut accurately to the shape of the cell which they fill, whether the edge be straight, curved or stepshaped. Beneath each garnet can be seen the piece of gold foil with its chequerboard pattern which reflects light back through the garnet at different angles. In this piece can be seen all the competent assurance of a firstrate craftsman. These objects, together with the many minor pieces of garnet jewellery found in the grave, *Plates 4–6* form the nucleus of a corpus of jewellery which has a local East Anglian character. Although related in a superficial manner to the garnet jewellery of Kent, the Sutton Hoo jewellery, together with a number of other pieces in the grave, was apparently made in a single East Anglian workshop under a number of influences, English, Frankish and Swedish.

The third group of objects comprises the symbols of royalty, an iron standard and whetstone, which may be considered as a sceptre. These objects have been studied comprehensively by Dr Berges and Dr Gauert. Here we can only describe them briefly and indicate their symbolism. The standard is made of iron, is about six feet four inches high, and consists of a long iron bar surmounted by a ring topped by a bronze-covered iron stag. At its foot is a barbed spike. Immediately below the ring are four short arms, each terminating in formalized bull's heads. About a foot below the ring is an iron grill with horned projections at the corners linked with iron bars to a point about halfway down the standard. At first it was thought that the object was a flambeau, or lampstand, but it seems more reasonable to suppose that it is in fact a standard (of the type known as *Tufa*) which Bede says was carried in front of King Edwin of Northumbria; the object is more or less unparalleled in the Europe of that time.

The whetstone found at Sutton Hoo shows no traces of use for any normal sharpening process; indeed the delicate carving and bronze casing at the terminals make it unlikely that it was ever intended to be used for such a purpose. Of square section, it is about twenty-four inches long and tapers towards the terminals. The looped terminals are painted red and enclosed in a bronze cage. Below the terminals, at each end and on each face, are a series of human masks carved in low relief. The whole stone is ground to a finely polished surface. This object is unparalleled in the Anglo-Saxon world, although a fragment of a large whetstone decorated with crude representations of the human face has recently been found at Hough-on-the-Hill in Lincolnshire, and two smaller whetstones carved with human masks have been found in the Celtic west. The fact that this whetstone has no conceivable use endows it with a significance of its own. The idea that it is a sceptre has received general acceptance: in the words of Sir Thomas Kendrick, 'Nothing like this monstrous stone exists anywhere else. It is a

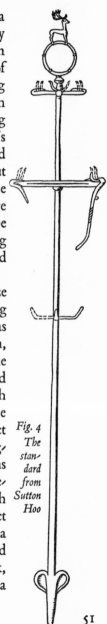

Fig. 4 The stan- dard from Sutton Hoo

51

Plate 10

unique, savage thing; and inexplicable, except perhaps as a symbol proper to the king himself and the divinity and mystery which surrounded the smith and his tools in the northern world.' Whether we accept it as a sceptre or as a wand of office and authority is immaterial; we have something here that is out-side the run of material normally found in Anglo-Saxon graves.

Lastly, mention must be made of objects of the utmost importance – the coins. There were thirty-seven coins, three blanks and two small ingots, all of gold, in the Sutton Hoo burial. They were originally enclosed in the purse, of which only the lid mounts survive. The coins were all *tremises* (one-third of a solidus, the standard imperial gold coin of the Roman Empire) and were all struck in France. A close and detailed study of the coins by Mr Grierson has dated their deposition to between the years 650 and 660. This date is therefore the date of the whole burial.

There can be little doubt that the man who was commemo-rated by the burial of such elaborate grave-goods was a royal personage, and presumably a king. It would seem likely that he would be an East Anglian king, a member of the Wuffingas dynasty, who died between 650 and 660. It is hardly likely to have been a foreigner, for a cenotaph such as this would surely have been set up in the homeland of the king. Three kings fulfil the conditions laid down; Anna, who died in 654, Aethelhere, who died in the following year, and Aethelwald, who died in 663 or 664. Aethelwald's successor did not die until 713 and Anna's predecessors were joint kings, who died about 640. The first possible king, Anna, was buried in the monastery at Blythburgh. Aethelhere died in battle, his body being lost in the flood waters of the Winwaed. We do not know what happened to Aethelwald's body. Both Anna and Aethelwald were Christians and presumably Aethelwald, like Anna, received a Christian burial. Aethelhere was a pagan, a lapsed Christian. Now, it is possible that the followers of either

Anna or Aethelwald erected this cenotaph to their master as a sort of insurance policy, in the event of Christianity failing to furnish him with sufficient provision in the after-life, and indeed Anna has been suggested as the subject of this burial. My own view is that the Sutton Hoo cenotaph commemorates Aethelhere, the pagan king, whose body was not available to his followers when they erected his grave. In this heroic age, one of the greatest things a man could do was to die on the field of battle. Aethelhere, despite his short reign, died the death of a hero and would therefore be deemed worthy by his followers of receiving the burial due to a pagan hero. We shall never know the answer to this problem – the unknown king has left his memorial and we can only admire the riches and glories of these East Anglian kings who numbered among their treasures the finest jewellery produced in Europe at that time, as well as riches imported from the exotic Mediterranean world. The king who was commemorated by this burial must be seen as the peer of any Germanic or Saxon king in Western Europe.

Chapter II

Christian Antiquities

596: In this year Pope Gregory sent Augustine to England with a good number of monks, who preached God's word to the English people.

Thus, laconically, does the *Anglo-Saxon Chronicle* dismiss the Christian mission to England. The conversion of England was a long process; it was many decades, for example, before pagan burial practices ceased completely. Gradually, as Christianity became more effective, grave-goods became of less importance in contributing to our knowledge of the Anglo-Saxons and a different class of antiquity takes their place. Churches, chalices, crosses and manuscripts replace the pots and brooches, the swords and the jewellery of the illiterate pagan population. The church brought with it Mediterranean learning and ideas; it brought writing and architecture, sculpture and painting to add colour and sophistication to the life of the English.

Christianity was not unknown in England before the advent of St Augustine; in the north there was a submerged but active Celtic church, founded while the Romans still ruled the country. Missionaries of this church travelled from Scotland and Ireland to the Continent, apparently leaving the Saxon invader to his own gods and his own beliefs. In Kent, King Aethelbert had married a Christian princess, Bertha, the daughter of the Frankish king Charibert, and she had brought with her a Frankish bishop named Liudhard. But it was Augustine who was to convert Aethelbert and Kent. The slow and tedious business of the conversion of England then began in earnest and perhaps the greatest triumph of the mission was the conversion of King Edwin of Northumbria in 626.

For the missionaries, however, it was uphill work and there were many setbacks before England was finally converted.

We have few, if any, relics of pre-Augustinian Christianity in Anglo-Saxon England. There are a number of churches of Roman date in this country but only two churches, or fragments of churches, now survive which were used in the period between the departure of the Romans and the Augustinian mission, and the evidence for their use is slender. The first is the church of St Martin at Canterbury where a portion of the chancel may be part of the ancient church which Queen Bertha had used before the arrival of St Augustine. Dr Fletcher and Mr Jackson have recently suggested that the church at Lydd, which still stands, may perhaps have been part of a pre-Augustinian basilican church, of a type best paralleled in Rome at the Porta Maggiore; there is certainly a strong case for assuming that this is a sub-Roman or late Roman structure.

One of the principal sites of the conversion has recently been found in the excavations at Yeavering, Northumberland. Yeavering was the site of one of the palaces of Paulinus's royal convert, the Northumbrian king Edwin. The preliminary report draws attention to the most remarkable feature found on the site, namely traces of a large timber grand-stand resembling in plan the triangular *cuneus* of a Roman theatre. This was almost certainly the meeting place, or moot, of the local assembly and it is tempting to imagine Paulinus preaching from the platform at the focus of the structure. We must await Mr Hope-Taylor's final report on his excavations, but buildings were certainly found on the site that can only be interpreted as churches, while one of them was possibly a pagan temple which had been converted to Christian use.

The architectural aspects of the Anglo-Saxon church are best summarized by the description of three churches, two from the period immediately following the conversion and one from the later period, towards the Norman Conquest. All the surviving Anglo-Saxon churches, with one exception, are built of stone. The one exception is the much restored late church at Greenstead, in the wooded county of Essex, which is built of vertical timbers in the manner of the Norwegian churches of the early medieval period. There were traces of what might have been a timber church at Yeavering, and from the literary sources we know of timber churches at Lindisfarne, Glaston-bury and Chester-le-Street. Recent excavations by Mr Olof Olsen inside medieval Danish churches, built of masonry, have revealed traces of earlier churches built in wood, and it is possible that investigations of English churches built after the Conquest of imported stone in a wooded or fen area might reveal similar traces.

Fig. 5   The church of St Peter and St Paul at Canterbury was founded by St Augustine soon after his arrival in England. He died in 604, before it was completed. Excavations in the early years of this century revealed a fairly complete ground-plan. It was the church of a monastery of which the ancillary buildings have disappeared. It was an important church, designed, as we know from Bede's *Ecclesiastical History,* to be the burial place of kings and archbishops and was presumably much grander than the normal building of the period, although in the general details of its construction it falls into line with other South English churches. The church, which was built almost entirely of re-used Roman brick, consisted of a nave flanked by side chapels, a narthex or entrance hall, and a chancel, every trace of which has disappeared. One of the side chapels was dedicated to St Gregory, another to St Martin. It contained the tombs of St Augustine and some of his successors at Canter-bury as well as the tombs of Aethelbert and his queen Bertha. The church was about twenty-seven feet wide but its length cannot be ascertained. As must be expected, the ground plan of this church reflects its Italian prototypes, although the form of the chancel in English churches of this plan is possibly a

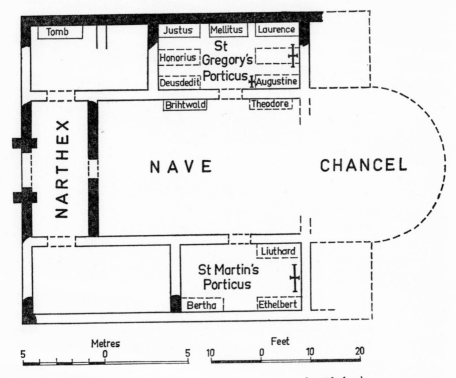

Fig. 5. Ground-plan of church of SS. Peter and Paul, Canterbury (after Clapham)

Byzantine rather than a Roman form.

Markedly different from the rather early southern group are the Northumbrian churches of which that at Escomb, County Durham, is the best surviving example. It is built of neatly-dressed squarish stones in regular courses and has an over-all length of 53½ feet. Its square chancel takes up ten feet of this length and is joined to the nave by a high, narrow arch, constructed of large stones running through the whole thickness of the wall. The voussoirs are wedge-shaped with plain chamfered imposts at the springing level. The sides of the opening

Plate 13
Fig. 6

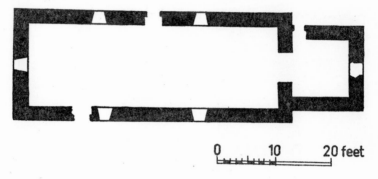

0 ___ 10 ___ 20 feet

Fig. 6. Ground-plan of Escomb church, Co. Durham (after Clapham)

are constructed of large, long, narrow stones alternately set at right angles to each other (this type of work must not be confused with later, mainly decorative, 'long and short' work). The windows of the church are either round or square headed, with an internal splay which enabled the minimum of glazing to admit the maximum amount of light. The original doors are square headed and the church is entered from the side. The date of this building is uncertain but it seems reasonable to assign it to the seventh century. It is interesting to note that the ground-plan of this church is closely related to that of one of the buildings found at Yeavering. Sir Alfred Clapham tentatively suggested that these churches of Northumbria, so different from those found in the south of England, are of Gaulish inspiration. We know that Benedict Biscop, one of the greatest religious leaders of the seventh century in Northumbria, brought stone-masons from Gaul, but as Clapham has so rightly pointed out, there is not enough evidence from either side to support this hypothesis; in fact it seems more and more unlikely in the face of the Yeavering evidence of a very early church of this plan.

Plate 12   The church at Earls Barton, Northamptonshire, exhibits features of the period after the Viking raids, which may be used

here to illustrate the differences in architectural detail between the earlier and later phases of Anglo-Saxon Christianity. Similar features can also be seen on many Anglo-Saxon churches, as for example at Wing in Buckinghamshire, and at Bradford- on-Avon, Wiltshire, which are illustrated here. The tower of Earls Barton church is probably one of the most spectacular surviving fragments of pre-Conquest architecture in this country. The nave and chancel of the church have disappeared, but it has been suggested that they must have been fairly small and insignificant. The tower, however, is impressively built of plastered rubble work and is decorated with vertical pilaster strips and horizontal string-courses, arcades and prominent long and short work (in which long stones are set, alternately upright and flat, at the corner of the building). The string- courses and the pilaster strips, derived from churches of the Carolingian Rhineland, are, with the triangular headed lights and the windows splayed both externally and internally (as distinct from the single internal splay of the Early Saxon period), clear and definite features of late Anglo-Saxon church architecture. In the topmost stage of the tower (other than the recent crenellation) can be seen the arcading built up on baluster shafts with the marked central swelling which is so common a feature of Anglo-Saxon architecture of the late period. The earlier pillars of this sort, like those at Bede's monastery of Monkwearmouth which was built in the late seventh century, are more often of regular cylindrical form. Most late Anglo-Saxon arches are round-headed and only such small openings as narrow doorways and windows have tri- angular heads which are copied from Carolingian examples. The windows of the churches were sometimes glazed. It is recorded, for example, that Benedict Biscop imported glaziers from Gaul. A tower such as that at Earls Barton fulfilled a multitude of functions; it not only served to hold bells, it was a strong point, a place of refuge in the face of attack and a store

Plate 14
Plate 15

house for the more precious possessions of the landowner. The fortress-like tower of the Anglo-Saxon church is the part of the building which most often survives, and, in its way, this fact is perhaps as indicative as any other of the state of restlessness of the later Saxon period.

This summary description of Anglo-Saxon church architecture can be nothing more than a quick sketch of a well-documented subject and the reader is referred to the general bibliography for further information on the matter.

Benedict Biscop imported not only glaziers, but also masons. We have seen how the pagan Anglo-Saxons had built in wood and regarded the stone building of the Romans with awe as the 'cunning work of giants'. It is significant that the Christian church, with its Mediterranean background, re-introduced the art of the mason into this country and with it the art of the stone carver. There must be nearly 2,500 known fragments of Anglo-Saxon sculpture in England and South Scotland, and, although many of them are decorative architectural features, a good many of them take the form of crosses and tombstones. The large stone crosses, sometimes eighteen feet high, which occur especially in the north of England, must be taken as marking preaching places or meeting places. It has been suggested that, when a community could not afford to build a church, a cross of wood or stone was erected and made the centre for Christian worship. There is a certain amount of evidence for this argument, despite the fact that many crosses are so rich that a small wooden church could have been built for the same price and in the same time as it would take to raise a cross. From the literature we learn that Willibald, who later became the missionary bishop of Eichstätt, was taken as a sick child 'to the cross of the Saviour, it being the custom of the Saxon people to erect a cross for the daily service of prayer on the estates of good and noble men, where there was no church.' The surviving crosses nearly all stood in a churchyard, and

such of them as do occur in the market-place of a town, as at
Sandbach in Cheshire, were presumably removed there at the
period of the Reformation. Even when there was a church
they would be used as a centre for preaching. St Oswald of
Worcester, for example, in the tenth century, frequently
preached near a memorial cross to congregations that were too
big for his church. Such crosses as that from Bewcastle in
Cumberland, or Ruthwell in Dumfriesshire, form part of a
large group which occurred, to use Sir Thomas Kendrick's
words, 'as a comprehensible advertisement for the Bible story'.
It is conceivable that in some cases the crosses were erected to
replace a wooden cross put up by the original missionary of the
area, as a commemoration of the conversion, but such theories
are incapable of proof. Many of these crosses were overthrown
during the Reformation; an Act of Assembly of the Church of
Scotland, for instance, dated 1642, ordered the 'idolatrous
monuments at Ruthwall' to be demolished.

Plate 53

Memorial crosses and tombstones vary considerably in size
and shape. Some memorial stones, such as the so-called pillow
stones from Hartlepool, were actually buried in the grave; they
are square and bear a cross with the name of the person who
was buried engraved on the surface. Others, the hog's-backed
tombstones of the north-west of England, for example, are
recumbent stones with the shape of a pitched roof. The vast
majority took the form of crosses or slabs, sometimes as much
as ten feet high, erected as headstones on graves. The tombstones are immediately derived from Roman prototypes, which
are quite common in this country, and from the Celtic tombstones so often encountered in western Britain; they are certainly not a characteristic of the pagan Germanic forbears of
the Anglo-Saxons.

From literary sources we learn of the richness of church
treasuries of the Anglo-Saxon period. Between 970 and the
Norman Conquest the Abbey of Ely, for example, received

many gifts, including four silver-gilt figures of virgin saints, set with precious stones, a gold crucifix, many silver and gold crosses, one at least bearing a figure of Christ, a shrine deco- rated with gold and precious stones to hold the relics of St Wendreda, a life-size seated figure of the Virgin and Child in gold and silver, an episcopal cross, a silver ciborium in the shape of a tower, chalices, patens, censers and a large quantity of rich textiles. Many of these objects disappeared when the monks of Ely paid William the Conqueror a fine in 1074: on this occasion the figures of the four virgins, the figures of the Virgin and Child, crosses, altars, shrines, book-covers, chalices, patens, bowls, buckets, chalice-pipes, cups and dishes were sacrificed to raise the required one thousand marks. Such objects rarely survive: but two great finds allow a glimpse of the trappings of the Christian Church. The first is the Coffin of St Cuthbert, and the second the Trewhiddle Hoard.

On 17th May 1827, a party of clerics and workmen gathered in the feretory of Durham Cathedral to open the reputed grave of St Cuthbert, who had died in 687 at his hermitage on Farne Island. The shrine of the saint had been pillaged at the Reform- ation and a very circumstantial account survives of the break- ing-open of the coffin and its reburial by Henry VIII's Com- missioners. Happily the body of the saint, with the light wood- en coffin dating from the seventh century, survived with some of the other contents of the coffin until the nineteenth-century opening of the tomb. The members of the Cathedral chapter, when they opened the tomb, found not only the skeleton of St Cuthbert and relics of other saints, but certain objects placed in the tomb either at the time of his original burial or at one of the many later re-openings of the tomb during the early Middle Ages. Only five objects of a date roughly contemporary with St Cuthbert survive: these are the pectoral cross of the Saint, the portable altar, the comb, a gospel book and the coffin itself.

Plate 40   The pectoral cross, which has a span of 2¼ inches, is of gold

inset with garnets in a cell pattern made up of adjacent rec﹨
tangles, with a circular garnet at the centre and a loop for
suspension. It is hollow, built on a base﹨plate; a cylindrical
collar in the centre carries the circular garnet which rests on a
white shell imported from tropical waters. The garnets in the
centre and those on the arms are bordered by billeted and
beaded edgings and by dummy rivets in the shape of small
cylinders of gold crowned by a golden granule. The cross is
remarkable in that it is a Christian object carried out in the
technique of the pagan Anglo﹨Saxon jeweller. Other crosses
in this technique are known from Wilton and Ixworth, and a
small pendant gold cross with a central garnet occurs in the
Desborough necklace. Taken together, these objects show that
there was no immediate change in the fashions of jewellery
with the introduction of Christianity, for they closely resemble
the garnet jewellery of the pagan period; but we shall discuss
this matter below.

Plates 41, 42

The portable altar of St Cuthbert is the earliest but not the
only, portable altar of the Anglo﹨Saxon period. Originally it
was a small block of oak forming a rectangle measuring
5¼ by 4¾ inches, inscribed IN HONOREM S PETRU ('In honour
of St Peter') and carved with five crosses, one in the centre and
one in each corner. Either during the Saint's lifetime or within
a few years of his death, a silver shrine was added to the altar,
enclosing it completely. The silver plates are decorated in an
embossed technique. On one side is a now fragmentary repre﹨
sentation of a seated St Peter. The back of the shrine bears
interlace and foliate patterns and the remains of an inscription
which cannot be interpreted.

Altars such as these would be carried by a priest or bishop on
his missionary journeys, and were apparently quite common.
Symeon of Durham tells us that a wooden altar was found at
the time of the mid﹨eleventh﹨century translation of St Acca,
Bishop of Hexham, who died in 740. It was made of two

Plate 16

pieces of wood fastened with silver nails and inscribed to the glory of the Trinity, St Mary and St Sophia. In the Cluny Museum in Paris is another Anglo-Saxon altar of porphyry, mounted on an oak base and bounded by strips of parcel-gilt silver. It is about 10¼ inches long and has a much worn nielloed inscription round the edge (niello is the black sulphide of silver). The silver border of the porphyry face is decorated with figures: at the top is a crucifixion between the symbols of St Luke and St John; below, the symbols of St Mark and St Matthew flank an *Agnus Dei,* and on the long sides are St John and the Virgin with the two archangels, Gabriel and Raphael. The back of the altar was covered with velvet held in place by small silver plates. It is of late tenth-century date. Larger altars do not survive, but we have descriptions in Anglo-Saxon literature of altar frontals, for instance the altar at Ripon, which was clothed in a rich purple textile worked with gold thread.

Also preserved in the tomb of St Cuthbert was a large ivory two-sided comb with thin teeth on one side and thicker teeth on the other. In the centre of the comb is a pierced hole and the central panel has one convex and one straight side. It is other-wise quite plain. The comb is probably contemporary with the Saint and, although the evidence for the liturgical use of the comb at such an early date is rather slender, there can be little doubt that it was used by the celebrant in the Mass, as was occasionally the practice in the later Middle Ages.

The coffin of the Saint is a light shell of oak carved in a linear style with representations of saints and archangels. It is discussed in greater detail below (p. 154).

Probably the most interesting of St Cuthbert's relics are the vestments, particularly the stole, maniple and girdle. Inscrip-tions on the stole and maniple tell us that they were made to the order of Queen Aelfflaed for Bishop Frithestan. Queen Aelfflaed died before 916 and Frithestan was Bishop of

Winchester from 909 to 931, so the vestments must have been made between 909 and 916. They were probably given to the shrine of St Cuthbert by Aelfflaed's stepson, King Aethelstan, about 934, for he is recorded as having presented various gifts to the shrine including a stole, maniple and girdle. Richly embroidered on the stole are the standing figures of the sixteen prophets, separated from each other by fronds of acanthus, and set on either side of a central *Agnus Dei;* the two ends bear busts of St Thomas and St James. The maniple bore a similar design except that the central figure is the hand of God, and the flanking figures are the Popes Sixtus II, Gregory the Great, St Lawrence and St Peter. The terminal pieces are decorated with busts of St John the Baptist and St John the Evangelist, all identified by inscriptions. The colours of these pieces of embroidery are now faded and it is difficult to distinguish them. Recent cleaning, however, has shown that as well as the gold thread which abounds, bluish-green, sage-green, delicate pinks, dark brown and dark green were all used. It was per-haps such a stole as this that we know was designed by St Dunstan for the Lady Aethelwynn to embroider a few years later. The interest of these pieces is mainly art-historical, as will be shown in a later chapter; in this context their importance lies in the fact that they are the only surviving examples of Anglo-Saxon ecclesiastical vestments.

The Trewhiddle hoard is for many reasons one of the most important finds of the whole Anglo-Saxon period. It was found in 1774 in an old mine-working at Trewhiddle, near St Austell, Cornwall, and contained, besides a number of coins which date its deposition to about 875, the animal-ornamented mounts of a drinking-horn, which ornament gives to the art of the period the name 'Trewhiddle style'. Most of the objects from the hoard are now in the British Museum. Its importance here lies in the fact that two objects of ecclesiastical use were found in the hoard, a silver scourge and a chalice. This is one

Plate 17

of the two Anglo-Saxon chalices that survive: it is five inches high, is made of silver, and was originally collared with a beaded wire above and below the knop in the manner of many of the chalices of the period. The chalice that was found in 1104, in St Cuthbert's tomb with a paten, no longer survives, but we must presume that it was similar to the gilt-bronze chalice found at Hexham, not far from Durham, at the end of the last century: it is small (only 2½ inches high) and is probably a travelling chalice, perhaps one used with a portable altar like that of St Cuthbert. It is similar in shape to the Trewhiddle

Plate 61

chalice and typologically is closely related to the great Tassilo chalice (some 10½ inches high), the chief treasure of the monastery of Kremsmünster in Austria. The Tassilo chalice was made for the monastery at the order of Duke Tassilo, between 777 and 788, probably by an Englishman or by a craftsman trained in an English school.

The second ecclesiastical object found in the Trewhiddle hoard – the scourge – is unique. Scourges are otherwise known only from literature. It is made of silver wire plaited in the Trichinopoly technique so familiar to school children, who to this day practise it under the name of 'tatting' with the aid of a discarded cotton reel.

No crook-shaped croziers of the Anglo-Saxon period survive although Irish examples and manuscript illuminations indicate their appearance. The head of a crozier of a rather later period, however, from the tomb of Bishop Ranulph Flambard of Durham (died 1128), shows that they do not differ greatly from the shepherd's crook borne by modern bishops. Croziers with a T-shaped or crutch head were also used and an early eleventh-century example of such a head, made of ivory, survives from Alcester. Another similar crozier of Anglo-Saxon manufacture is in the treasury of Cologne Cathedral.

A few other pieces of church plate survive. There is, for

Fig. 7. The Gandersheim casket. Brunswick, Ducal Museum (after Stephens)

example, a cruet in the British Museum which might have been used for ecclesiastical purposes. It is of cast gilt-bronze and probably dates from the early eleventh century. In the same style is a series of censer covers, one from Pershore, one from Canterbury and one from London Bridge. These three covers are cast in openwork and are square in plan with a gabled roof. The body of the censer was probably spherical and the whole object was, it seems, suspended on cords or on four thin bars which, running through the loops of the cover, allowed the top to be raised or lowered. This latter mechanism is to be seen in the illumination of a psalter, of eleventh-century date, in the British Museum.

The only surviving Anglo-Saxon altar cross is that from Bischofshofen, near Salzburg, known as the Rupert Cross. A much more splendid example is illustrated in the eleventh-century Register of the Winchester New Minster. A small eleventh-century cross, bearing an ivory figure of Christ, in the Victoria and Albert Museum and a cross in the treasury at Maastricht are all that survive of countless such objects.

Large numbers of Celtic reliquaries and shrines survive but Saxon reliquaries are rare. Two nielloed silver plates in the British Museum from a house-shaped casket probably formed part of a house-shaped shrine, of a type common throughout Europe. Similar pieces in boxwood and ivory of Anglo-Saxon manufacture are known in foreign collections, one of which, the Gandersheim Casket, is associated by a runic inscription with the Abbey of Ely. Another, once in the collection of Dr Nelson, is of boxwood and bears scenes of Christian significance. A third piece, a shrine from Mortain, France, has an inscription in English runic lettering.

It is recorded that Benedict Biscop beautified the church at Monkwearmouth with sacred pictures of figures from the New Testament, while the church at Jarrow had similar pictures together with some that were intended to illustrate the connection

Plate 79

Plate 18

Fig. 7

between the Old and the New Testaments. None of these paintings survives, and we have no idea what they looked like; but as we know of no other painting from this period other than traces of colour on tombstones and other carvings (as for instance on the famous Viking Tombstone from St Paul's churchyard in the Guildhall Museum, London), we can only lament that we may no longer see, as did Leland in the six teenth century, the brilliant painting of the cross-shaft in the church at Reculver, Kent.

Plate 74

The most magnificent remains of Anglo-Saxon Christianity are the manuscripts, often beautifully illuminated, which survive in considerable numbers. These are of extreme importance in our understanding of Anglo-Saxon art and will be discussed in that context in another chapter. In England the art of the scribe, working to the glory of God, often reached heights unequalled on the Continent and, just as the English craftsmen in Rome made church plate for the altar of St Peter's itself, so did English scribes work in the new monasteries of Germany and France. At the same time foreign craftsmen were at work in England. We have seen how glaziers and masons were brought to Northumbria by Benedict Biscop, and much later the pulpit and crucifix at Beverley were described as 'of Germanic workmanship'.

Traces of Christianity abound in secular contexts; the curse on the back of a large silver disc brooch from Sutton, Isle of Ely, bears God's name; the nose guard of the helmet from Benty Grange bears a cross in inlaid silver; the king who was commemorated at Sutton Hoo had a pair of spoons, symbolizing his christening, inscribed with the names Saul and Paul; the ring of Queen Ethelswith bears a representation of the Lamb of God. Angels appear on an ivory panel from Winchester and the hand of God appears on coins of Edward the Elder and other Anglo-Saxon kings. The impact of Christianity on Anglo-Saxon society and its importance in

Plate 78

Plate 75

everyday Saxon life are attested by these and many other similar representations of Christian symbolism.

CHAPTER III

The Life of the People

VILLAGES AND AGRICULTURE

THE ENGLISH VILLAGE is an Anglo-Saxon product. It is noteworthy that few existing English villages of the present day do not appear in Domesday Book, while hardly any of them have a Roman origin. Roman capitalism had produced the villa system and, despite Seebohm's argument for continuity between the Anglo-Saxon village and the Roman villa, there can be no doubt that the idea of the villa with its organized industry and agriculture was anathema to the individualistic Saxon. The Anglo-Saxon economy, of the pagan period at least, was based firmly on the village; the Roman towns and villas were to a large extent ignored.

The Anglo-Saxon of more humble station apparently owned his own land and farmed it in association with his fellow villagers. He lived in the village for protection and was surrounded by his own, and his neighbours', fields (isolated farmsteads were a rarity in Anglo-Saxon England). He farmed his land under the open field system, whereby every man had a number of strips scattered within the area of his village. Although such a system was not, and could not be, used in the less fertile parts of the country (in the marshes of Lincolnshire and the forest land of the Weald, for example), most of the inhabited areas would be farmed in this fashion.

Certain villages betray, to this day, their Anglo-Saxon ancestry. Dr Hoskins has quoted the Hertfordshire village of Bygrave as a typical example. The territory of the village was about 1,800 acres in extent and the houses were all grouped round the church. There were no isolated farmsteads in the fields, which were originally farmed on the strip system.

a

Fig. 8. Reconstruction of houses, etc. from Warendorf, showing a long house (a), various smaller buildings, barns, etc., and a hut of the type found at Sutton Courtenay. Berkshire (g)

Examples such as this enable us to gain some impression of the general appearance of an Anglo-Saxon village, but after a thousand or more years' use, the details of the Anglo-Saxon village plan have become blurred.

Unfortunately no Anglo-Saxon village has ever been completely excavated; fairly large numbers of sites have been partially investigated and have produced a considerable quantity of material (pottery, implements, etc.), as well as the ground-plan of a few timber-framed huts. Working under extremely difficult conditions, Mr Leeds uncovered a number of small huts at Sutton Courtenay in Berkshire. Other excavations at Crossgates, near Scarborough, at Sandtun in Kent and at St Neots in Huntingdonshire, for instance, have produced the plans of small rectangular houses which are little more than hovels and which date from both the early and the late Anglo-Saxon periods. Some of these huts had a sunken floor, the pitched roof coming down to the ground from a central ridge pole; huts

b

c

d

e

f

g

of this type must have been liable to flooding and extremely unpleasant to use. Some of them were almost certainly used as dwellings by members of the lowest class of society, but many of them were probably workshops. Two of the houses explored at Sutton Courtenay were certainly weaving sheds, a third was doubtless a pottery shed, and others also probably had specialized uses.

Comparison with such Continental sites as Lindholm Høje, near Ålborg in Denmark, Warendorf, near Münster in Germany and Tofting, in Holstein, Germany, has demonstrated that huts of similar form occur in the neighbourhood of larger longhouses. The groundplans of more than seventyfive buildings were uncovered at Warendorf, which is the most extensive village of its type yet excavated. Not all the buildings were, of course, contemporary with each other; some represent a number of successive rebuildings. But the excavators were able to recognize a village of rectangular dwellinghouses, some

Fig. 8

73

measuring as much as eighty feet by twenty-one feet, some very much smaller. Barns, stables, byres and other specialist buildings were also found. [The houses were wooden frame buildings with wattle and daub walls and thatched roof.] The later phases of the village of Lindholm Høje in Denmark show similar buildings, together with one of the extraordinary boat-shaped houses that are a feature of Viking Age Denmark. At all these places huts, of the same general type as those found at Sutton Courtenay, have been uncovered, and Mr Ralegh Radford has very rightly pointed out that Anglo-Saxon villages were probably very much like their Continental contemporaries, with long-houses as well as the small huts. Until such a village is found in England and excavated, students will have to rely on these Continental parallels and on vague generalizations based on literary evidence and the appearance of present-day villages.

The literary evidence concerning villages and houses is extremely complex: besides casual mentions in chronicles and biographies, there are charters describing estates and their boundaries, wills giving details of some of the furnishings of the houses, and even an early eleventh-century document on estate management which gives an account of the rights and duties of the various classes of society in relationship to the manor. From literature we can gain a vivid sense of the life of the village, and of the comfort of a great hall like that found during the Yeavering excavations. Archaeology has produced little more than a few house-plans and a few thousand wretched pots – things cold in their meaning and seemingly without relationship to people who actually lived more than a thousand years ago. For the moment the historian must provide the living picture of the Anglo-Saxon village – the archaeologist can only provide a little background.

[The study of Anglo-Saxon agriculture] has not received as much attention as it deserves. We know a great deal about

Fig. 9. Plough, from eleventh-century manuscript in British Museum (Cotton Tiberius B.V.f.3)

prehistoric, Roman and medieval agriculture, but few people have tried to gather the scattered Anglo-Saxon evidence together. Certain facts are known and can be simply stated. The most common cereals were barley, oats and wheat. Flax was grown for cloth-making and woad for dyeing. Fruit and nuts were probably gathered from the forest, and Parain has suggested that a few rough fruit trees were even planted deliberately on the edge of the forest. Tools were needed for these pursuits, but few have survived.

No plough, and only a single plough-share (from Westly Waterless, Cambs.), is known to have survived from the Anglo-Saxon period. From the manuscripts and the Bayeux tapestry we can glean a certain amount of evidence, which, however, must be treated with extreme care. An artist illuminating a manuscript would not necessarily go out in the fields and look at a plough before he drew it: he would be much more likely to copy a drawing from another manuscript, which may itself have been painted in Padua or Paris. The evidence for the English plough of the Anglo-Saxon period is, then, very slender, but certain suggestions as to its structure can be made. It was a fairly heavy implement drawn by a number of oxen; it had a heavy wheel, but no mould-board; the furrow was

Figs. 9, 10

75

Fig. 10a. Plough, from the Bayeux Tapestry

turned by a coulter which was shifted at the end of each furrow, so that the next furrow would lie in the same direction. The field would then be harrowed with an implement that may well have looked like the one shown in the Bayeux tapestry, and the seed scattered broadcast.

Fig. 10

Certain harvesting implements survive. Four scythe-blades were found at Hurbuck in County Durham, in a hoard of Anglo-Saxon tools. The blades were bound to the handle and the upturned point of the tang, which can still be seen on one of the Hurbuck examples, was hammered into the haft to give it greater security. These scythe-blades bear a striking resemblance to scythes illustrated in manuscripts. Sickles, bill-hooks and pitch-forks are also illustrated in the manuscripts, but none of these is known from Anglo-Saxon contexts. Spades were made of wood and were shod with iron. A few of these shoes have been found in archaeological contexts, including the example from Sandtun, an Anglo-Saxon village in Kent. Manuscript evidence would seem to imply that the blade of the spade was set at one side of the handle. Large numbers of axes used for forestry and carpentry survive. A series of these, with adzes, a pick and an auger, from Hurbuck, is illustrated here. The grain produced in the fields was milled locally. There was often more than one mill in a village; Hatfield in Hertfordshire,

Fig. 11

Fig. 12

Fig. 13

Fig. 14

Fig. 10b. Harrow, from the Bayeux Tapestry

for example, had four at the time of the Domesday survey. Not all the mills, however, would be as elaborate as the mill recently excavated at Old Windsor in Berkshire. This mill, which probably served the royal manor, had three vertical water wheels, working in parallel and turned by water flowing through a ditch dug for three-quarters of a mile across a bend in the Thames. The ditch, or leet, was twenty feet wide and twelve feet deep and was re-cut several times before it went out of use in the early eleventh century.

The pastoral side of Anglo-Saxon agriculture is even less well documented. Nobody has, for example, yet made an analysis of the animal bones found on Anglo-Saxon habitation sites. Sheep, cattle, pigs and goats were bred, probably in that order of importance. Wool was one of the main exports of Anglo-Saxon England and the cloth industry seems to have been extensive; all that survives in the archaeological record, however, besides the odd sheep-bone, is a few pairs of shears and a tool found at Sutton Courtenay, which might have been used for carding wool. Sheep and cattle were, of course, also kept for their milk and their meat: they would be fattened during the summer and the least promising beasts would be slaughtered in the autumn, the meat being preserved by salting or drying. Only the strongest cattle would be kept through the

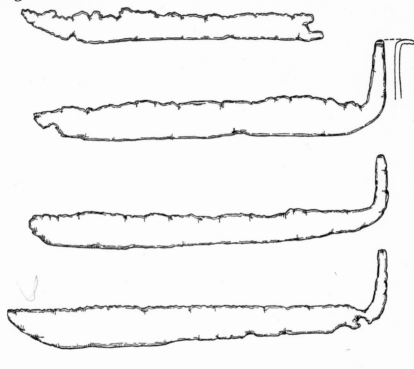

Fig. 11. Hoard of tools
from Hurbuck, Co.
Durham, including
scythe blades, axes,
adzes, an auger and
a small pick. London,
British Museum

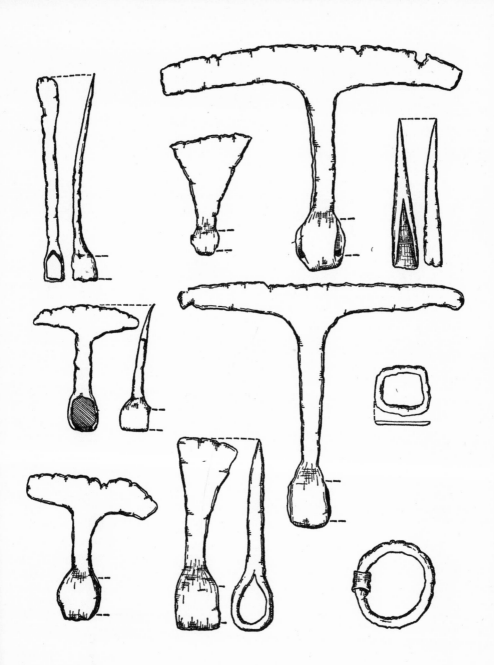

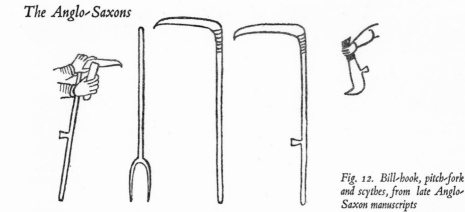

Fig. 12. Bill-hook, pitch-fork and scythes, from late Anglo-Saxon manuscripts

winter and, judging from analogy with medieval Denmark where the cattle were often so weak at the end of the winter that they had to be carried from the byre in spring, it was often touch and go whether they survived or not. Horses were luxury animals but certainly existed in some numbers and were used for draught as well as for riding.

TOWNS AND TRADE

Our knowledge of the physical appearance and even of the actual existence of Anglo-Saxon towns is, at least before Alfred's time, tenuous in the extreme. Excavations on sites bombed during the 1939–45 war, particularly in Canterbury and Southampton, together with recent research excavations at Thetford, Oxford, Cricklade and Wareham, have produced a certain amount of evidence which is unfortunately not yet published; any statement here must therefore be preliminary. We have, in an earlier chapter, mentioned the apparent desertion of the ancient Roman towns, but some remnant of Roman municipal government must have survived the Saxon invasions. The Saxon bishops who established themselves in Roman towns were, as Sir Frank Stenton has demonstrated,

conscious of the ancient origin of the town which they dis/
tinguished by the word *civitas* (city) – their brother bishops in
Anglo/Saxon foundations did not use this word. The existence
of Roman remains at Carlisle is attested in one of the Lives of
St Cuthbert, in a passage which implies a Saxon population in
a Roman town. By the time of Bede, as we have seen, the
ancient Roman city of London had become 'the metropolis of
the East Saxons, a mart of many people coming by land or sea.'
In 627 Paulinus came to Lincoln to evangelize the natives; he
converted the reeve, the royal official and chief citizen, who
built a church. Such references as these show that there was a
certain amount of administration in the ancient Roman towns
and that they were not all completely depopulated.

Some Roman towns, however, must have been completely
deserted. When King Offa founded the monastery in honour
of St Alban, the first British martyr, he gave the monks land
near the deserted Roman city of Verulamium. The buildings of
the ancient city served as a quarry for the monastery and, later,
for the town which grew up around it. In a similar way
Silchester and Wroxeter were quarried for building stone,
while a marble sarcophagus from Grantchester was re/used to
house the body of Queen Ethelthryth. Chester was still
deserted in 893 when a Viking army sheltered within its walls.
The Roman towns decayed, but in the ruins of some of them
Anglo/Saxon squatters huddled together for protection.
Miserable huts sprang up in Canterbury, which was shortly
to become the centre of a royal court and a town of increasing
population, in which it was soon necessary for local customary
law to forbid the building of houses too close to each other.
The street plans of such towns as Gloucester, Colchester and
Winchester reflect the street plan of the Roman city, but the
collapsing Roman buildings often forced the inhabitants of the
towns to make new paths round the debris, thus creating a new
lay/out.

*Fig. 13. Man using
spade; notice the
suggestion of a shoe
at its point (after the
Bayeux Tapestry)*

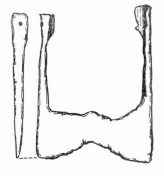

Fig. 14. Fish-hooks, draw-knife and shoe of spade from Sandtun, Kent. London, British Museum

Gradually most of the Roman towns were repopulated and other towns, probably little more than overgrown villages, were fortified. These new towns occurred only when economic and geographical conditions were favourable, or when defence became necessary. From a very early stage the defence of a town was, with the building of bridges, an important communal obligation, a duty from which even the favoured church was not excused.

As most of the Anglo-Saxon towns have been built over by their medieval and modern successors, it will be only over a long period of time that the archaeologist can investigate their structure. Such investigations depend mainly on demolitions connected with rebuilding programmes or enemy action. But a few towns still survive within the earthen banks of the Anglo-Saxon burgh. One of these is the ancient port of Wareham in Dorset, which was probably first fortified by King Alfred in the ninth century when a rectangular bank and ditch was thrown round it. Wareham was a town of some importance and early Celtic inscriptions and remains of Roman habitation would seem to indicate that it was already old in Alfred's day. Two of the Saxon churches survived until the middle of the last century, but now only St Martin's church, against the north wall, and the encircling bank and ditch remain to indicate the Anglo-Saxon character of the site. St Martin's is a small church, but Lady St Mary's, which was destroyed in 1842, was much larger; indeed pictures and plans show that it was one of the largest surviving Anglo-Saxon churches in the country. In the Saxon period it was of sufficient importance to be the burial place of Beohtric, King of the West Saxons, and the temporary resting-place of King Edward the Martyr, who was murdered at nearby Corfe in 978. The bank and ditch which formed the defences of the town were much altered in the twelfth century and the ancient form of the bank, with its palisaded or stone embattled top, although interpreted by excavation nearly ten years ago, has never been published, so that archaeologists must remain ignorant of one of the most important sites of the Anglo-Saxon period. Similarly we must also await the report on the Anglo-Saxon town at Thetford, with its many houses and churches, its pottery kilns and other industrial remains.

But archaeology can give some idea of the function of an Anglo-Saxon town, even if our knowledge of its physical appearance is tenuous. The town served two primary functions in the Anglo-Saxon period; first as a defence and administra-tive centre, and secondly as a market and economic centre. The defences of Wareham illustrate the former function to perfec-tion; within these walls men could live in comparative safety in the troubled periods when pirates and raiders were abroad. From the *Anglo-Saxon Chronicle* we have an interesting picture of the native inhabitants of Winchester in 1006, pro-tected by the town's fortifications, watching from a distance the Viking host marching with their booty to the sea. Not only would the inhabitants of a town benefit from its fortifications but the people from the surrounding countryside would be able to take refuge there in time of trouble. The fortification of thirty-one Wessex towns in the time of King Alfred means, as Sir Frank Stenton long ago pointed out, that in Wessex no village was more than twenty miles away from a fortified centre.

But it is the economic function of the town that leaves most trace in the archaeological record. Exotic materials – precious stones, glass, bronzes, mill-stones, silver vessels, coins and many other objects – found in Anglo-Saxon contexts are indicative of the primary function of a town: trade. The towns were not only markets for agricultural produce from the surrounding countryside, they served also as markets for goods from abroad. Although most of the trade must have been carried out by means of barter, the presence of a coinage of extremely high standard indicates a medium of trade more normal to civilized communities.

It was not until the late seventh century that the first Anglo-Saxon coins were struck. The hoard from Crondall in Hampshire, deposited about 670, is particularly important in this context. It contained, besides two pieces of jewellery, 101 gold coins of which seventy-three are some of the earliest surviving Anglo-Saxon imitations of Roman and Merovingian coins. Gold was not destined to remain the metal of currency for very long; it was to be replaced by silver, but the struggle to retain the gold standard is reflected in a number of coins struck in electrum (an alloy of gold and silver). By the early eighth century, however, the Anglo-Saxons had adopted the silver coinage which was to remain the basis of all trade until the fourteenth century.

The earliest silver coins were, despite various attempts to maintain a high standard, often degenerate and debased in weight and legend. The factor which above all others was to influence Anglo-Saxon coinage for the better was the appearance in Northern Europe of a very large number of Arabic coins at the end of the ninth century. The coins appear partly as the result of Viking raids into Russia and the Near East and to a certain extent as the result of trade between Western

Europe and the East. The Arabic coins found in Scandinavia and Germany are mostly of silver. Already about 780 Offa had taken over from Kent a new coin, the penny. Towards the end of his reign Offa standardized the weight of the penny at twenty-two grains and it rarely dropped below this figure for nearly five hundred years.

The English coinage was essentially a royal institution, although the archbishops of Canterbury and York were allowed to strike their own coins. The actual coining, however, was done in many provincial centres, presumably under the control of the reeve or other royal official. The privilege of striking coins was farmed out to a professional moneyer, whose name usually appears on the reverse of the coin. The penalties for debasing the coinage were extremely heavy and were presumably strictly enforced, for base coin is rarely found. It has already been noted that, in Edgar's reign and in the succeed-ing reigns, the coinage was called in and reissued at regular intervals. Similarly all foreign money, which came into the country in the last two centuries of the Anglo-Saxon period, was melted down and re-struck. In this way the king could retain the standard of his coinage with no cost to himself, for the moneyer would buy coins for reminting by weight and not by face value. This interest of the Anglo-Saxon kings in keep-ing up the standard of the currency, made English coinage a recognized medium of exchange from the Balkans to Scandi-navia.

We have already mentioned a few of the more exotic im-ported materials which have been found in Anglo-Saxon contexts, and which must have reached this country by way of trade. This trade was carried on by people of all countries, but three nations seem to have dominated the trade of Europe for long periods of time – the Frisians, the Jews and the Arabs. The Frisians, who lived on the fertile shore of Holland, practi-cally controlled the trade of Northern Europe. They were a maritime people who had colonies in London and York and travelled between the great Baltic ports of the Viking Age, Birka, Haithabu and Schiringshal, carrying thither Rhenish wine, English and Frankish weapons, hunting dogs, oriental silks and English cloth, to barter for ropes, amber, furs – fox, beaver, sable and ermine, – and slaves. The Jews and the Arabs controlled the trade in Southern Europe, Asia and Africa. Ibn Khordadbeh describes one Jewish merchant thus: 'This merchant spoke the Arabic, Persian, Latin, French, Spanish and Slav languages. He travelled from the Occident to the Orient, sometimes by land and sometimes by sea. From the West he took eunuchs, women slaves, boys, brocade, beaver-skins, marten-pelts, other furs and swords.' He started in Western Europe (in the Frankish lands) by the Western Sea and travelled by sea to al-Farama (Pelusium in Egypt); then, changing his mode of transport on various occasions, he travelled by way of Arabia to India and China. On his return journey 'he bore with him muscat, aloes, camphor, cinnamon and other products of the East and returned with them to Constantinople.' This was but one of a number of journeys of like character made by this man; it reminds us that the international trade of Europe in the Dark Ages was extensive and that the trade connections of many of the merchants of this period would have put many a modern business house to shame.

But the Frisians, Arabs and Jews were not the only merchants: Anglo-Saxons were also trading with the Continent: 'I go on board my ship', says the merchant in Aelfric's *Colloquy*, 'with my freight and row over the regions of the sea, and sell my goods and buy precious things which are not produced on this land, and I bring it hither to you with great danger over the sea and sometimes I suffer shipwreck with the loss of all my goods, barely escaping with my life.' He describes the goods he brings back, 'purple and silk, precious gems and gold, rare garments and spices, wine and oil, ivory and brass, copper and tin, sulphur and glass and suchlike things . . .' English merchants traded hunting-dogs, furs, silver, linen, slaves, horses and weapons with Italy, and entered into trade agreements with the kings of Lombardy. The merchant bought and sold where and when he could; the type of cargo he carried with him was conditioned only by economic considerations. He had to contend with tolls and taxes, embargoes and customs officials; there is ample evidence of all these mercantile hazards in the documentary sources, while more direct piracy was also a very present danger, particularly in the Viking Age.

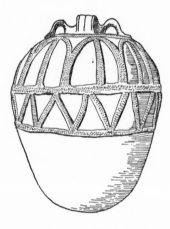

Fig. 15. Relief band amphora *from the Rhineland. Fragments of vessels of this type appear in English contexts. Scale about* $^1/_{12}$

The trade in perishable goods, which formed such an important part of the Anglo-Saxon mercantile system, is reflected in certain instances in the archaeological material. While we cannot hope to trace archaeologically the chief exports of Anglo-Saxon England – wool and cloth, – certain imports have left their mark. The occurrence of Continental pottery in England has already been mentioned. From the seventh century onwards we have evidence that pottery was imported from the Continent, which must presumably be associated with

Fig. 15 the German wine trade. The great relief-band *amphorae,* some of them three or four feet in height, can have been used for no other purpose than transporting wine. The wooden barrels *Fig. 16* which are depicted on the Bayeux tapestry and which presumably contained French wine have not left any trace in the pre-Conquest archaeological material, although remains of an immediately post-Conquest example have been found at Pevensey Castle.

The Eastern trade is reflected in such objects as the Egyptian glass found in an Anglo-Saxon grave in Sussex. Other fragments of Eastern glass in the Christian Anglo-Saxon period come from London, Chichester, Yorkshire and Fife. Also from the East are bronze bowls of Coptic origin, imported from Alexandria, garnets from India, and cowrie shells from the Indian Ocean, which tell us that mercantile contacts with the Orient were not casual. But apart from the occasional fragments of Oriental silk, we have no traces of spices and dyes and other perishable goods which the East could provide for the peripheral islands of the world.

TRANSPORT

One of the chief legacies of Rome was a system of roads, built so that Roman armies and merchandise could move quickly about the country. These well-constructed roads were used by the Anglo-Saxons in their ordinary day-to-day business. There can be little doubt that they deteriorated during the Anglo-Saxon period, but the volume of traffic was by no means as heavy as that in later medieval, Tudor and Stuart times, and the roads must have been in fairly good condition. The speed with which armies moved across country adequately reflects the condition of the roads.

The Anglo-Saxons apparently thought of the roads not, as the Romans had done, as a system of trunk communications, but as a means of communication between market towns.

Fig. 16. Cart, containing a barrel, drawn by two men The Bayeux Tapestry

Small tracks were developed from the newly-founded villages linking the village directly with the nearest town or with the nearest stretch of made road. Along the roads passed messengers and parties of clerics, royal officials and pilgrims, pack-animals and carts carrying merchandise, and the baggage train of the royal court as it moved from centre to centre.

There is but little archaeological trace of these means of transport. Pieces of horse-harness and, from Howletts, the only authenticated Anglo-Saxon horse-shoe are all that survive. No traces of the carts that figure in the manuscripts and in the Bayeux tapestry remain. Both two- and four-wheeled carts are *Fig. 16* represented in the manuscript sources and they appear to have been drawn by men as well as by draught animals. Farm carts had bodies of light staves (and perhaps of wickerwork). The wheels were spoked and made up of composite felloes. Travelling wagons, which would make longer journeys, were probably more substantially built and roofed with leather.

Whenever possible, however, merchandise was transported by water. This was quicker, less physically exhausting and cheaper. The Northern European practice of boat burial, to which we have already referred, has preserved for us the plans

Fig. 17. The Sutton Hoo ship

Fig. 17

of three boats. They all date from the seventh century and were all three found in Suffolk – one at Snape and two at Sutton Hoo. They were all rowing-boats: the largest and most com-plete example was that found at Sutton Hoo in 1939. The tim-bers of this boat had decayed until nearly all the actual body of the wood had disappeared, but the excavators skilfully isolated the marks left in the soil by the decaying wood and the iron clench nails which fastened the strakes to each other, and were able to plan and photograph the complete vessel. The ship was over 80 feet long and 14 feet in the beam; the prow rose to a height of at least 12½ feet above the level of the keel-plank amidships. It was a rowing-boat and, when lightly loaded, would have drawn about two feet of water. There were nine strakes on each quarter. To the wash strake, or gunwale strake, were attached thorn-shaped rowlocks. The keel was little more than a thickened plank. The ship was strengthened with twenty-six ribs, which were nailed only at their ends, pre-sumably being lashed to cleats on the strakes. There was no trace of the steering oar, which normally occurs on the star-board side of ships of this period.

No sailing-ships of this period (the seventh century) survive either in this country or on the Continent. We do not even know whether they existed or not. However, we do know that by the eighth century sailing-ships were in use in Northern waters and that oars were only a secondary method of propul-sion. A number of Viking ships have been excavated in Norway and it is reasonable to presume that English boats, of the ninth century at least, were of a similar form, with a proper keel, thirteen or fourteen strakes and a footing for a mast. The ship found at Gokstad in Norway is not dissimilar to those depicted some 250 years later on the Bayeux tapestry and in the pages of the latest Saxon manuscripts, with their rising prows and sterns and large square sails set on a central mast. Smaller boats of the Anglo-Saxon period have not been found in England, although river-going rowing-boats have been found on the Continent. These smaller boats are often miniature editions of the sea-going vessels, but we must presume that skin boats and coracles were also used by the fishermen who lost their fish-hooks at Sandtun in Kent.

Fig. 14

DRESS AND PERSONAL ORNAMENT

No fragment of ordinary Anglo-Saxon dress, of more than a few square inches in size, survives. Our whole knowledge of dress has therefore to be built up on the evidence of a few clothes found in Danish bogs, on pictorial evidence and on literary sources. The Anglo-Saxon literary sources provide us with precious little information, and that of the most casual sort: an English missionary bishop, for example, freezing as a result of a German winter, sends home a *cri de cœur* for a new cloak. Another cleric, Alcuin, sends to a friend on the Continent for garments and hoods of goat-hair. In Frankish sources we have fuller descriptions of dress. Charlemagne, for example, took a patriotic pride in dressing in the native costume of the Franks. Einhard tells us that he wore some sort of linen combinations beneath his trousers and a woollen three-quarter-length tunic, trimmed with silk and belted at the waist. His shoes, which were buckled over his feet, had bands attached to them, with which he cross-gartered his legs. He wore a fur cape, which appears to have been fairly short but covered both the front and the back of his body. Over all this he wore a long, flowing mantle, fastened at the shoulder by a brooch.

Dress of more or less this same form seems to have been worn

Fig. 18. Clothes portrayed in eleventh-century manuscripts

generally in Western and Northern Europe from the Roman period to the Conquest. A long-sleeved tunic and a pair of trousers of a style similar to that described by Einhard have been found in the peat-bogs of southern Jutland as well as a square cloak of wool with a fringed edge. The trousers were supported by a leather belt threaded through loops, and the socks were sewn on to the ends of the trouser legs. The clothes portrayed in the later Anglo-Saxon manuscripts correspond in most details to those described by Einhard and to the garments, some five hundred years earlier in date, found in the Danish bogs as well as those portrayed on the late seventh-century Franks Casket. Tacitus says that the dress of the Germans consisted of a tunic, fastened with a thorn or a brooch, and a mantle and nothing else. This seems to be true of the poorer elements of society in the late Anglo-Saxon period, if the manuscript evidence can be trusted. We can reasonably suppose that men's

Fig. 18

Plate 56

dress remained more or less unaltered in form throughout the Anglo-Saxon period, only varying in quality and richness.

Strangely enough, women's dress also changed but little. According to Tacitus, the German women of the Roman period wore very much the same sort of dress as the men, save that they 'often wear undergarments of linen, embroidered with purple, and, as the upper part does not extend to sleeves, forearms and upper arms are bare'. We must assume that the women did not wear trousers. The women's tunic and cloak were apparently longer than those of the men. Towards the Conquest the dress developed long, open sleeves, although a hundred years earlier sleeves gathered at the wrist are depicted in certain manuscripts. Hats were seldom used by men, whose hair was usually worn long, while women wore a more or less voluminous hood.

The commonest garments were made of wool of a quality which varies, in the words of Mr Lethbridge, 'from . . . the texture of a modern flannel shirt to that of Harris tweed', while linen has been well attested on a number of occasions: silk was imported from the Orient, but presumably only by the extremely wealthy. We have no clue as to the colours with which these fabrics were dyed, although the ladies who embroidered the stole of St Cuthbert used threads of pastel shades as well as those of more brilliant colour. Many of the garments had braided edges. In the Taplow barrow, for example, wool and gold were woven together – in a tablet weave – to form the edging of the cloak, or tunic, of the warrior buried there. Even in more humble context the cuffs of a tunic were woven in tablet weave (without the gold thread); an example of this was found by Mrs Crowfoot in the material from a grave from St John's College, Cambridge, cricket field. There is also a suggestion that the cuffs found in the Sleaford, Lincolnshire, cemetery were of leather (which might indicate a leather tunic).

Although jewellery is rarely seen in Anglo-Saxon manuscript illustrations, it is obvious from the large number of brooches and other jewellery found in the graves of the pagan period that the Anglo-Saxons delighted in decking themselves with knick-knacks. No other subject in Anglo-Saxon archaeology has received so much attention as the brooches; they are a typologist's dream. It is often forgotten, however, that brooches were integral parts of everyday dress in the days before buttons. Basically there were three types of Anglo-Saxon brooch, the ring (or penannular) brooch, the bow brooch and the disc brooch. The ring brooches and penannular brooches are derived from pre-Roman Celtic forms and, until the seventh and eighth centuries, are often rather plain, apart from occasional more exotic examples. In the Northumbrian and Irish areas, in the eighth and ninth centuries, penannular brooches with large expanded terminals were developed. The terminals were decorated with animal ornaments in the style of the period. Another type was evolved with spherical, brambled terminals.

More commonly found are the various types of bronze bow brooch, which developed from the Iron Age and Roman safety-pin type of brooch, under a certain amount of Eastern European influence. These take many forms, some simple and others more elaborate. The great square-headed brooches (some of which are made of silver) and the cruciform brooches are often as much as six inches in length, while some of the so-called 'small-long' brooches are barely two inches in length. The square-headed brooches are often decorated with chip-carved ornament (e.g. the example illustrated in fig. 31); cruciform brooches are often plainer in form. The brooch, with the main ornamental elements, was cast and then touched up with chisel and punch. The catch plate and hinge lugs, which carried the spring-pin, were then brazed on the back, while the face of the brooch, if it were a particularly grand example, was gilded. This type of brooch probably died out towards the end

Plate 20

Fig. 19

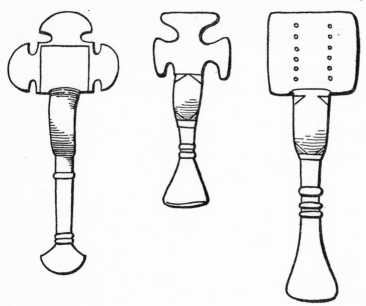

Fig. 19. Small long-brooches from Stapenhill, Staffs, Rothwell, Northants, and Icklingham, Suffolk

of the pagan period.

The third type of brooch, which is of circular form, has Roman precursors. There are many forms of circular brooch: some are merely plain bronze discs decorated with ring and dot or other mechanical ornament, while others have a silvered or tinned surface. More elaborate are the cast and gilded saucer brooches, which have a Rhenish ancestry. The richest disc brooches are, of course, the great polychrome jewels of Kent, which are discussed at some length below (p. 138). In the Christian period disc brooches are found which are sometimes very elaborate objects of silver and gold. They are usually dished like a watch glass, and the largest is more than five inches in diameter.

Plate 21

Plates 35–38

Brooches of other forms naturally occur; small brooches in the shape of birds and animals were adopted by the pagan Anglo~Saxons from Continental models, a silver trefoil brooch of eighth~century date from Kirkoswald in Cumber~ land is perhaps the precursor of a long series of similar brooches manufactured in the ninth and tenth centuries by the Vikings, while in the Christian period brooches in the shape of a cross are not unknown.

Plate 62

The smaller brooches (saucer brooches, small~long brooches, etc.), are usually found, in pairs, in women's graves; they were apparently worn on either side of the tunic above the bosom, and, occasionally, festoons of beads were suspended between them. The large brooches are usually found singly and were probably used to fasten the cloak, or mantle, at the shoulder. This method of fastening the cloak can be seen illustrated in various manuscripts and sculptures. Apparently these larger brooches were worn by both men and women.

Necklaces of glass beads, amber and even, occasionally, beautifully shaped amethyst drops are quite common in Anglo~ Saxon graves. They are never illustrated in manuscripts but, from their position in the graves of the pagan dead, it seems that they were usually worn as festoons either pinned or sewn to the garment above the breast. Now and again more splendid neck~

Plate 33

laces of gold or garnet are found, as, for example, at Des~ borough in Northamptonshire, where a series of gold pendants and gold~mounted cabochon garnets, with an equal~armed cross in the centre, is spaced by a series of barrel~shaped gold beads.

A chatelaine with imitation keys – T~shaped pieces of flat bronze, known as girdle hangers – and possibly a double~sided bone comb would hang at a woman's waist. Her hair might be done up with a jewelled fillet or be adorned with small rings of bronze. She would occasionally wear ear~rings of bronze or silver and even a finger~ring. The braided cuff of her tunic might be fastened, if she lived in East Anglia, with a pair of plates of a rather elaborate hook-and-eye form and, if she were wealthy, she might have jewelled ends to her girdle. Bangles of silver, bronze or glass might be worn on her arm, and even on her leg; a small bronze drum-like needle-case might also hang at her waist. A fairly wealthy farmer's wife might wear a great deal of jewellery and would probably look most colourful. Her husband's sword belt, which hung over his right shoulder, might have a large ornamented buckle, but if he were too poor to own a sword he might have a buckled belt at his waist, attached to which would almost certainly be a sheath bearing a small wooden-hilted knife.

POTTERY

As with most archaeological periods, the pottery of the Anglo-Saxon people forms a very large part of their material remains. The wheel-turned pottery of the Roman period, with the whole system of commercial potting, disappeared, to be replaced by a mud-pie type of hand-made pottery which was introduced by the new Anglo-Saxon settlers. The vessels were made of local clay, probably by the women of the village, and were fired in the domestic fires or in rough-and-ready kilns, which have left no archaeological trace.

First let us examine the pottery of the pagan period. Some of the pottery, such as that found in the Anglo-Saxon graves at Sleaford, is featureless and ugly. Other vessels found elsewhere are obviously the product of a skilled potter and were sought-after over wide areas; the 'Icklingham' potter's wares, for instance, are found all over Cambridgeshire and Suffolk (at Lackford, Icklingham, Girton, Cambridge, West Stow Heath, etc.). The difference is explained by the fact that while the Sleaford pottery was ordinary everyday ware, filled with food or drink and placed in the inhumation grave to provide for the buried man's journey into the after-life, the ware of the

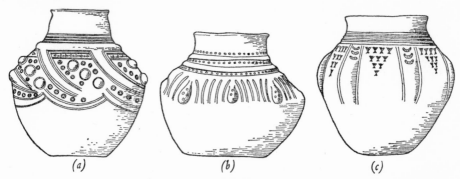

(a)   (b)   (c)

Fig. 20. Anglo-Saxon pottery: (a) Hough-on-the-Hill, Lincs; (b) South Elkington, Lincs; (c) Barton Seagrave, Northants

Fig. 20
(a), (b), (c)

Icklingham potter was specially made to contain the ashes of the dead – the difference, say, between a modern soap-box and a modern coffin. Quite often a domestic vessel might be adapted as a funerary urn, but many of the pots, such as that illustrated in fig. 20(a), were obviously made as funerary vessels.

Typical Anglo-Saxon pottery has a paste varying between black and grey-brown. It is hand-made and the ware is so soft that a finger-nail easily bites into it. Much of the finer funerary ware is decorated with largish, oval bosses or impressed stamps and incised lines – very occasionally animals are drawn and stamped on the vessel, but such occurrences are rare and the design is usually purely ornamental. Certain decorative features of the funerary pottery have been interpreted as of ethnic significance, and successful attempts have been made to link similar types of pottery in England and in the Continental homeland of the Anglo-Saxons; but, in the light of the mixed nature of the Anglo-Saxon population at the time of the settle- ment, extreme caution is necessary in any consideration of the origins of the people who used this pottery in England. Basically speaking, the Anglian pottery in the Continental homeland is decorated with simple horizontal linear motifs round the neck, above a zone of vertical ornament sometimes

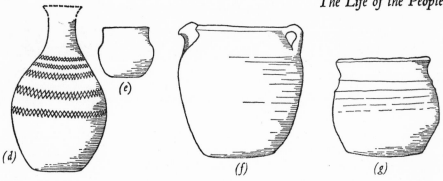

Fig. 20. Anglo-Saxon pottery: (d) Kent; (e) Sleaford, Lincs; (f) and (g) Ipswich, Suffolk

interspaced with small bosses on the shoulder of the pot. The Saxon pottery is decorated with elongated bosses, sometimes of complicated form, below the shoulder of the pot, and vertical slashed or stamped ornament. The pottery of North-Western Europe and England reflects the community of the area, but it is difficult to sort out in detail the different relationships within that community.

A different type of pottery is found in Kentish graves: flask-shaped, it is usually red to buff in colour. Its form is probably based on that of Roman wine bottles and it may well have been made abroad in the Rhenish area and be the sole surviving fossil of the Continental wine trade of this early period. Coarse pottery of the normal Anglo-Saxon type rarely occurs in Kent.

Fig. 20 (d)

Pottery, of the type found at Sleaford, is found in cemeteries and on pagan settlement sites all over England and occurs in such late seventh- and early eighth-century contexts as at the monastery of Whitby; while pottery of a similar form, though turned on a slow wheel, is found in eighth- and ninth-century contexts in East Anglia and elsewhere, as, for example, on the site of the Savoy palace in London. Our knowledge of this later pottery is drawn mainly from East Anglia. The primitive kiln – little more than a circular depression of puddled clay –

Fig. 20
(f), (g)

Fig. 15

found in Carr Street, Ipswich, in 1928, has given the name of Ipswich to this type of eighth- and ninth-century pottery (which is also known as Middle Saxon pottery); it is hard, sandy and greyish-black in colour. The pots have thick walls and sagging base and are occasionally decorated with a stamped ornament. Three forms are found: the simple cooking-pot, which is directly descended from the vessel of the pagan period found at Sleaford and elsewhere, a spouted pitcher and a bottle.

At some stage in the Middle Saxon period the use of the fast potter's wheel was introduced. Some of the pottery found at Ipswich, for example, demonstrates this fact. In the late Saxon period a far more accomplished pottery is found, known as Thetford ware after the Norfolk town where it was found in such profusion. Three kilns were excavated at Thetford, but have not yet been published. They produced a variety of shapes: pitchers, angled bowls, large storage jars (some as much as three feet high), water-bottles and lamps. The pottery is apparently influenced by Rhenish prototypes, such as the relief-band *amphora*. Closely allied to the Thetford pottery is St Neots ware (so called after the town in Huntingdonshire) which is grey-purple in colour, with a soft fabric containing much crushed sea-shell. The commonest types of this ware are bowls with flanged rims and various forms of cooking pot.

From Stamford, Lincolnshire, comes the most individual type of pottery of the Anglo-Saxon period; it is known as Stamford ware since a kiln was found there in 1875. Existing accounts of this kiln are not complete enough to indicate whether it was pre- or post-Conquest in date, for this pottery continued to be made long after the Norman invasion. The clay of the estuarine deposits in the Stamford area produced a fine creamy-grey pottery, which sometimes has a pinkish tinge. Spouted pitchers, jugs, jars and deep flanged bowls of this ware are found as far apart as Oxford and York. One of the most distinctive features of this pottery is that it is glazed in a light green or yellowish shade – the first glazed pottery to be seen in England since the Roman period. It is not known where the practice of glazing originated. It is possible that kilns were operating in Dutch Limburg at this period and producing this type of pottery, but there is no evidence of priority of dating on either side of the Channel. It is reasonably certain that the practice of glazing pottery was not invented in Western Europe: it was probably introduced from the Near East – glazed pottery is known from Persia and Byzantium.

The pottery from the south of England, from Kent to Dorset, was at this period little different from the Middle Saxon pottery. Generally speaking, where Stamford ware and Continental pottery are not found, the local pottery consisted mainly of bag-shaped cooking pots, sometimes decorated with irregular scratches. Vessels of this form are found well on into the twelfth century. Pottery of this period from the north of England and from the Midlands occurs rarely. The examples that are found are mainly derivatives of East Anglian wares.

GLASS

One of the most important groups of material found in Anglo-Saxon graves is the series of glass vessels which add a touch of lightness to the generally ponderous aspect of Anglo-Saxon antiquities. The forms produced by the Anglo-Saxon glass-blower, and his opposite number on the Continent, may have been stereotyped and the colours may not have been as rich as those used by the Romans but, compared with vessels of other material found in the Anglo-Saxon period, the variety of form and the attractive colours (yellows, greens, browns and blues) are extremely refreshing.

Fig. 21

Anglo-Saxon glass has been the special study of Dr Harden, and his work must form the basis of any summary of the subject. A fairly large number of Roman glasses (nearly thirty) have been found in Anglo-Saxon graves; particularly notice-

Fig. 21

able are the cone beakers such as that from Kempston in Bedfordshire. Glass of Anglo-Saxon type, made both in Britain and on the Continent, is found in some profusion. The commonest forms are the squat jars and the palm cups; less common are the bag beakers, and only two examples are known from this country of glass drinking-horns (both from Rainham, Essex). These rarer types, as well as the slightly more common, but hideous, claw-beakers, were almost certainly manufactured on the Continent and imported into this country by the wealthy. It is a noticeable feature that many of the glass vessels found in graves of the pagan period will not stand up-right – a feature which can be observed in the later manu-scripts, and in the Bayeux tapestry, where glasses are seen to lie and not stand on the table.

No glass kilns of the pagan Anglo-Saxon period are known to survive, but certain glasses, as, for example, the palm cup, are found in such quantities that they were very probably made in this country and it has been suggested that a glass house was situated somewhere in the neighbourhood of the richest of all Anglo-Saxon cemeteries, that at Faversham in Kent. The only glass kilns known in England were found recently at Glaston-bury, Somerset. Under the north-east corner of the later medi-eval cloister were found the remains of the floors of three kilns. Fragments of glass, found in association with them, indicate a date in the ninth or tenth centuries. One of the kilns produced very few fragments of glass and it may be possible to interpret it as an annealing kiln. We must await the publication of these kilns, but we seem to have here the remains of the only known Anglo-Saxon glass factory in this country. We must presume, on the analogy of later glass houses, that all the kilns were under the same roof and that the glass-blowers, using tools not very different from those used today, produced their glass vessels in the area between the kilns.

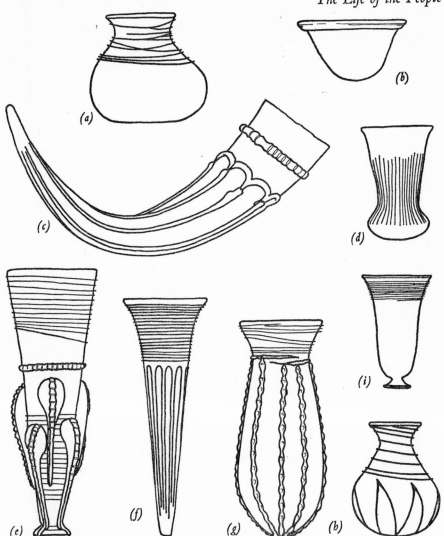

Fig. 21. Anglo-Saxon glassware: (a) squat jar, Upchurch, Kent; (b) palm cup, Faversham, Kent; (c) drinking-horn, Rainham, Essex; (d) bell beaker, Ashford, Kent; (e) claw-beaker, Taplow, Bucks; (f) cone beaker, Kempston, Beds; (g) bag beaker, Faversham, Kent; (h) pouch bottle, Sarre, Kent; (i) stemmed beaker, Croydon, Surrey

CHAPTER IV

Weapons and Warfare

THIS WAS A HEROIC AGE: the vernacular literature makes this abundantly clear. Even Christ is seen as a heroic Prince:

Then the young hero, God Almighty,
Firm and unflinching, stripped himself.

The greatest virtue was loyalty to one's lord: the warrior shared the spoils of battle, but he was also willing to die for his lord – indeed it was considered a disgrace to leave the field of battle if one's chief were dead. This spirit is reflected in both the poetry and prose of the Anglo-Saxons long after Christianity had become firmly established in England. War has left its remains in the archaeological record, in the form of innumerable weapons buried in the graves of warriors and peasants. It is fitting that when we deal with a heroic age we should consider these remains at some length.

Although the sword was the most important Anglo-Saxon weapon, it is not found with the frequency of other weapons in the graves of the male Anglo-Saxon. Baldwin-Brown, a long time ago, quoted some figures to demonstrate the comparative rarity of swords: two were found in the 308 graves from Kingston, seven came from the 150 graves at Bifrons, although at Sarre there was one sword in every ten graves. To these figures may be added some more modern results: one sword was found in the hundred graves excavated at Holywell Row and none at all in the 123 graves found at Burwell. We know from the documents of the Christian Saxon period that swords were precious objects, handed down from father to son. We have already noticed that the sword which had belonged to Offa was bequeathed by an eleventh-century prince to his brother. Again and again we meet references in Anglo-Saxon poetry to swords which have greater virtue because they were old, or because they had belonged to some famous person of the past.

The sword was the weapon of the man of wealth and position. Some swords, as for example Beowulf's sword, *Naegling*, even bore names of their own. Few of these rich swords survive; at best, all that remains is a few mounts of bronze, or of more precious metal, which embellished the hilt. Now and again an exceptionally rich sword occurs to give us an impression of the wealth and position of its owner.

Plate 2

The earliest Anglo-Saxon swords, those of the pagan period, are two-edged and about two feet six inches long; they are thin-bladed with straight edges and rather rounded points. Known technically as a *spatha,* the Anglo-Saxon sword of the pagan period has a long and continuous ancestry that stems back to the Celtic La Tène sword, which is of similar length and shape. The sword was carried in a scabbard, which was usually made of two thin laths of leather-covered wood. The mouth of the scabbard was sometimes ornamented with a metal band; one of the most impressive examples, from Chessel Down, has a gilt-bronze ornamented pattern on one face and a magical runic inscription on the back. Some scabbards were bound with a strip of metal and were tipped with a metal chape, which occasionally, as at Brighthampton, was ornamented. The scabbard was sometimes lined with fleece, and this has been explained by the fact that the natural greases of the sheep's wool would keep the blade from rusting. Professor Atkinson was able to undertake a thorough examination of the scabbard of a sword from Petersfinger. It was made up of alternate layers of wood and leather, a thin wooden sheet on the inside, wood on one outer face and leather on the other, all bound round the edges with bronze. At Brushfield in Derbyshire, Thomas Bateman found a scabbard which was covered with leather ornamented with a series of lozenges, while a fragment of a similar scabbard was found at Hexham in

Plate 25

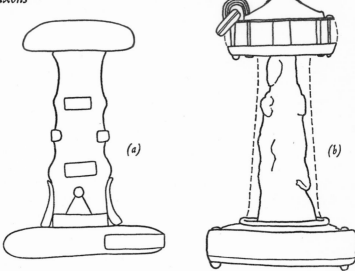

Fig. 22. Schematised drawings of sword hilts: (a) Cumberland (seventh century);
(b) Gilton, Kent (sixth century); (c) no provenance (Viking); (d) Abingdon (ninth
century—see pl. 22)

Northumbria. The blade of the sword was comparatively thin
and was occasionally decorated with a stamped design; two
boars, for instance, appear on the blade of a sword from the
River Lark. Some blades are 'pattern welded'. This method of
twisting bands of iron together and beating the resulting plait
into a thin blade which is then edged with hard steel, adds
flexibility to an otherwise comparatively intractable weapon.
The face of the sword is then polished and the marbled effect
achieved must be responsible for such passages as the description in *Beowulf:* 'Upon him gleams the ancient heirloom, the
hard, ring patterned sword, treasure of the Heathobeards.'
Often, however, the blade is beaten out of one piece of metal
and is unornamented.

Fig. 22
    The hilt has been used by Behmer and others as the basis of a
typological distinction between the various swords, but as yet

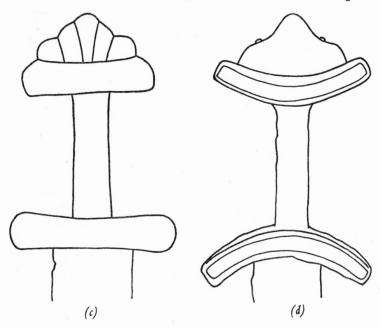

(c)   *(d)*

no really satisfactory typology has been evolved (Behmer's type
1, for example, includes swords of both the fifth and seventh
centuries). The hilt is built up round the tang which is a con-
tinuation of the blade. The guard, or quillions, consists
usually of a simple insubstantial rectangular block of bone or
wood, projecting an inch on either side of the blade. The grip
is of wood (less frequently of bone) and is bound with cloth or
leather, or even with silver wire or cord. Occasionally, as on a
sword from Chessel Down, the grip is decorated with ornamental metal plates. The tang is riveted over a plate at the top of
the hilt, and, to cover the rather rudimentary result, a pommel
is often added which can be highly decorative. This pommel
can take many forms; a sword found in a grave in the Fleam
Dike, in Cambridgeshire, for example, has a spherical pommel; sometimes it is merely a very flat triangle of iron, but more

often it has a sub-triangular shape, which has long rejoiced in the picturesque description of 'the cocked-hat pommel'. Some cocked-hat pommels are decorated with small rings, a few of which are free-running rings, while others are immovable and merely decorative. This feature, which in England is rare and largely confined to Kent, is a universal trait throughout North-ern Europe and one is reminded of the passage in the Old Norse *Poetic Edda:*

> *I know of swords lying in Sigarsholm . . .*
> *One among them the finest of all . . .*
> *A ring on the hilt, valour midway*
> *and fear on the point for him who wins it.*

The ring, as has often been pointed out, is associated with the heroic quality of courage.

The early type of sword, the *spatha,* with its miserable hilt, apparently continued to be made well on into the Christian period; drawings in Carolingian manuscripts show us swords of similar form. But about the end of the eighth century, with the advent of the Vikings, an entirely revolutionary sword was developed in Western Europe – perhaps in Britain, perhaps in the Rhineland. We have in this country some fifty or sixty swords of this period, some of which were obviously weapons of the Viking invaders. They vary considerably in quality and size; most of them have blades which are between two feet six inches and two feet nine inches in length, have broad shallow fullers (a fuller is a groove running down the centre of the blade) and are pattern welded; the best are well-made, springy and double-edged. The rather pathetic hilt of the *spatha* is replaced by a more splendid one with fine projecting quillions, which may be straight or curved. The pommels can be divided roughly into two typological groups, one having a lobed shape and the other a flattened semicircular, or pointed oval, cap; a few types fall into neither category.

The blades of these later swords are much stronger and

heavier than those of the *spatha*. Occasionally, inlaid or etched into the blade is the name of the swordsmith who made them, and many swords found in Scandinavia, for example, bear the name of one of the great Anglo-Saxon swordsmiths, *Ulfberth*. As the hilts of some of these swords are not of Anglo-Saxon type the blades must have been imported into Scandinavia and mounted in a fashionable Viking hilt. Sometimes the blades have a magical inscription, as on the sword from Canwick Common, Lincoln, now in the British Museum, which has an inlaid silver inscription: ANTANANANTANANTAN.

Some of the Anglo-Saxon hilts are very grand; for instance, the parcel-gilt silver pommel from Fetter Lane in the City of London, decorated with whirling snakes interspaced with a leaf pattern, is one of the most beautiful and accurately executed pieces of metalwork to have survived from this period. Slightly less grand is a sword from Abingdon, Berkshire, which has silver plates inlaid into both the quillions and the pommel. The silver plates are decorated with animal, plant and even human motifs engraved and set with niello. There are parallels to the Abingdon sword from the River Witham, near Lincoln, from Dolven, Gronneberg and Hoven in Norway. Poor relations of these rich hilts are those from Yorkshire, Gooderstone, Norfolk, and Kaupang, Norway. The quillions and pommel are usually of iron, overlaid occasionally with silver but often merely decorated with a punched ornament; sometimes how-ever they are of bronze, as, for example, the pommel-guard from Exeter which bears the name of the maker in the Latin inscription LEOFRI/MEFE (Leofric me fecit, Leofric made me). It would seem that swords with lobed pommels and curved quillions were more elaborately decorated than the simpler D-shaped type, but this is perhaps a dangerous generalization. As most of the swords of this period found in England are casual finds, we know less about the scabbard than we do for the earlier period. However, traces of wood and

Plate 24

Plate 22

Plate 23

Fig. 23

109

Fig. 23. Sword pommel guard from Exeter, inscribed with name of maker (Leofric). London British Museum

rather elaborate chapes and mounts from scabbard openings indicate that they were little different from their pagan fore-runners. The sword hung at the left hip, being carried in a sling which passed over the right shoulder. The late Saxon type of sword continued in use well on into the Norman period.

Fig. 24

Related to the sword is the single-edged long-knife – the *scramasax*. Such knives were used by the men who murdered Sigibert in 575. Gregory of Tours described them as 'strong knives, commonly called *scramasaxes,* smeared with poison'. This statement has presumably been responsible for the un-doubtedly false assumption that the grooving on the blades of the *scramasaxes* held poison. The term *'scramasax'* covers a multitude of knives from the very short knife, no more than three inches long, to the considerable weapon which may be as much as two and a half feet in length. Here we shall concen-trate on the weapons only.

Plates, 26, 27

The typical *scramasax* of the Migration period, as found on the Continent, is a clumsy object about fifteen inches in length with an asymmetrical tang, though occasionally, as at Pouan, the weapon is as much as twenty-one inches in length and has a beautifully decorated hilt. *Scramasaxes* do not appear in this country until the latter part of the pagan period and their variety of shapes makes it difficult to generalize concerning them – for instance, one of the *scramasaxes* found at Uncleby in Yorkshire is twenty-four inches in length, while others may be as little as fourteen inches long. They were carried in a sheath at a man's thigh and the sheath was suspended from the belt by means of a series of small bronze loops; a very good example of this feature was found in the Marina Drive cemetery at Dunstable, Bedfordshire. The guard of the *scramasax* is often very insignificant, while the pommel

Fig. 24. Warrior portrayed in late Saxon manuscript (British Museum, Cotton Tiberius, C.VI)

can vary considerably in shape, from an unobtrusive 'cocked hat' to the more elaborate silver pommel of the Winchester *scramasax*; this is tripartite with a central lobe flanked by two shoulders which, in their design, are reminiscent of animal heads. An important, though later *scramasax* pommel, comes from Windsor, the central lobe of which is inlaid with a gold panel covered with interlaced filigree wire ornament, the thicker wire terminating in exquisite animal heads, while bunches of

Plate 27

grapes made of small granules of gold enrich the design even further.

The tradition of the pagan *scramasax* continues through into the Christian Saxon period: the *scramasaxes* from Ofton and Hoxne in Suffolk and from the Thames at Wandsworth may well belong to the eighth century. But the true late Saxon *scramasaxes* are typified by two fine examples in the British Museum, one from the Thames and the other from Sitting-bourne in Kent. The Thames *scramasax* is twenty-eight inches long and has an inlaid mosaic along its upper edge made up of copper, bronze and silver wire in triangles and lozenges. Also inlaid is the whole of the *futhorc*, or runic alphabet. The Sittingbourne *scramasax* is ornamented with inlaid panels decorated with the pure, vigorous Winchester art style which cannot be dated much before the middle of the tenth century; it carries the name of both its owner and its maker, Sigebereht and Bjorthelm. Many other *scramasaxes* of this later group are inlaid with copper or bronze wire and in fact the technique continues into the thirteenth century. It would be best to think of these *scramasaxes* as daggers, although many of the later, larger weapons may well have been more useful as a sword.

The commonest weapon of defence, of which traces are found in Anglo-Saxon graves, is the shield. The Anglo-Saxon shield comprises a round wooden board, known as an orb, with an iron boss in the centre. The orb is sometimes covered with leather and a central hole allows the knuckles of the hand to manœuvre within the hollow formed by the boss, the grip being attached at this place. Some of the shields were bound at the rim with a metal binding, but this is rare and a leather binding was presumably more common. The shields vary in size. The smallest shield recorded in England is one of twelve inches in diameter found at Petersfinger, Wiltshire, and the largest, thirty inches in diameter, came from Ringmer, Sussex. Traces of the orb are rarely found in Anglo-Saxon

Plate 26

Fig. 25

graves and these figures must be treated with caution. At Caenby, Lincolnshire, however, part of the orb of a substantial shield survived; it must have been at least an inch thick and was decorated with a series of gilt-bronze plaques decorated with interlace ornament. Judging by the few examples where the handle and the boss have been riveted together through the orb and where the wood has survived, it would appear that pagan Anglo-Saxon shields were often not much more than half an inch in thickness – in fact, not unlike the surviving Viking shields found in the Gokstad vessel in Norway which have a large and surprisingly thin orb. Such a shield would be light and easily handled in battle.

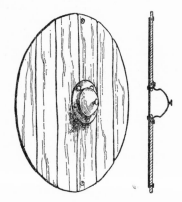

Fig. 25. Reconstructed Anglo-Saxon shield (after Wheeler)

The orbs were usually made of lime wood and were sometimes covered with leather, as at Sutton Hoo; the orbs of some shields would be painted, as in the Viking Gokstad find. All the surviving shield bosses are made of iron and are of three main shapes, one with concave sides and a carination, one with convex sides, and one conical. They are riveted to the orb through the flange, sometimes with bronze or gilt-headed rivets. They are usually beaten out of a single lump of metal, but occasionally, as in the Melbourn cemetery, a conical shield boss was made by bending a flat sheet of metal to form a cone. The boss is usually tipped with a button which can sometimes be elaborately decorated with a silver or bronze plaque.

There has been considerable discussion as to whether the shields were curved like a watch glass. It has been said more than once that, 'The angle of the boss flange indicates a considerable curvature to the surface of the shield.' Such an argument may well be false. The angle of the flange of the boss is probably an accident of manufacture, as it would be considerably more difficult to produce a boss with a flat flange, as distinct from an angled flange, because of the stresses in the metal. At the same time an angled flange would provide a better grip on the wood when the rivets were fastened. So very few complete shields have survived that the evidence is not conclusive. In the whole of Northern Europe, however, not a single curved shield orb has been found. There is some evidence that the orb of the Sutton Hoo shield was curved, the long attachments of the grip apparently providing for a curved board; similar evidence has been put forward in favour of curved shields in Italy and Germany. Detailed examination of the grip of one of the shields from Petersfinger, Wilts, has convinced the excavators that the shield was curved, with a radius of curvature of about twenty inches. The structure of this shield is of great interest, Professor Atkinson having shown that the shield orb was 'built up of two or more thicknesses of wood with the grain of one lamination running at right angles to the next, as in modern plywood'. He suggests that this structure was necessary in building up a convex shield, and that the orb was made up of a number of narrow strips laid side by side. The nineteenth-century description of the find of a shield at Linton may perhaps be illuminated in the light of the Petersfinger example: 'Enough was preserved to show the form to have been cirrcular, and laths of wood converged from the extremity to the umbo. These laths were fastened to the body of the shield, probably of wood, with twine.' The precise meaning of this description is obscure, but it has a remarkable coincidence with the description of the Petersfinger shield and it is possible that these shields were conical or curved. There can be little doubt therefore that curved shields were used by the Saxons and this is confirmed by manuscript illustrations.

Fig. 26

Fig. 26. Shields, spear-heads and battle axes, illustrated in Anglo-Saxon manuscripts

The shield and the spear were the common arms of the average soldier, and it is probable that some shields were made of wood and leather alone and that only the richer members or the community had shields with an iron boss. At Oberflacht in Germany, for example, an oval wooden shield covered with leather and without a boss was discovered. Tacitus, writing or the Germanic peoples at the beginning of our era, describes shields of wickerwork. It is not impossible that the Anglo-Saxons occasionally copied this form of construction. Most of the Anglo-Saxon shields illustrated in the contemporary manuscripts are round, while most of the shields illustrated in the Bayeux tapestry are kite-shaped. While it is probable that the Norman ladies who executed this giant labour were not particularly concerned with the shape of their opponents' weapons and followed the Norman fashion, it is not impossible that, despite the manuscript evidence, the Anglo-Saxons used kite-shaped shields in the eleventh century. One thing that emerges from the manuscript and tapestry evidence is that the shield of the late Saxon period was already being used for some sort of heraldic display. We cannot be sure that the signs on the shields indicated anything more than sympathetic magic or personal artistic taste, but it seems probable that certain signs indicated a clan or a sept.

'*Arma, id est scutum et lancum*' (a man's arms are the shield and the spear) say the laws of Charlemagne, and the ordinary Saxon must have fought mainly with these two weapons. Iron spearheads are the commonest weapon found in Anglo-Saxon contexts, yet, probably because they are so uninterestingly uniform, these have never been studied with the thoroughness accorded to other weapons. But the spear, not only a weapon of war but an implement of the hunt, is found both in the poor man's grave and, as at Sutton Hoo, in the grave of the king. The weapon of Woden was used universally and some of the finer spearheads decorated with inlaid precious metal indicate something of the value of this weapon in the mind of the Anglo-Saxon.

Our knowledge of the Anglo-Saxon spear, from the archaeological point of view, is based on the iron tips or heads and on the iron ferrule. The tip is usually leaf-shaped and has a

Fig. 27

socket for the shaft. It is usually lozenge-shaped in cross section, the blade rising from the edge to a medium rib, while the socket which continues from the narrow neck of the spearhead is split on the side and usually carries an iron rivet. Presumably

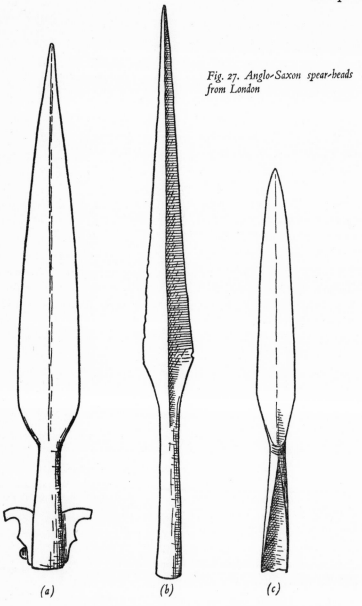

Fig. 27. Anglo-Saxon spear-heads from London

(a) *(b)* *(c)*

when the spearhead was fitted to its shaft, it was first riveted into place and the head made firm by hammering the socket so that the split end closed slightly, tightening the grip on the shaft.

Occasionally, as at Sutton Hoo, the spearhead is barbed, and spearheads of similar shapes are seen in later Saxon manu-scripts. Such barbing may be a development of the later Saxon period. The shaft, according to the literature, was usually made of ash. Now and again this socket is decorated by being inlaid with silver, copper or bronze – or sometimes by faceting.

Spearheads vary considerably in length, from a few inches to two feet and, though some have very prominent shoulders, the form varies very little throughout the Saxon period. In some cases the blades are pattern welded but this is an un-common occurrence. Lunate grooving of the blade on either side of the midrib has often been taken as a sign of Saxon workmanship, a technique that may perhaps have its roots in the Early Iron Age, where there are technical parallels. One of *Fig. 27 (a)* the late features, and one which is often called Carolingian, is the two wings, or spikes, which stick out on either side of the socket. These wings are functional in that they prevent the head of the spear from piercing the target too far, making with-drawal easier. These features can be noticed in a number of manuscripts from the ninth century onwards and are not without parallel in more modern contexts. From the manu-*Fig. 26* scripts it appears possible that these wings were not always fixed to the socket; some may have been made of wood and attached to the shaft. No complete Saxon spear survives; the nearest parallel is provided by the German grave-field at Oberflacht where an entire spear was found lying outside the coffin in which the warrior was buried. The spear was about seven feet long and the head was attached to the shaft by gilt-headed nails and further bound by a leather thong. This example agrees well in length with the spears illustrated in the

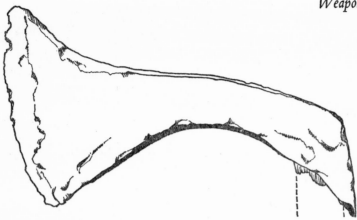

Fig. 28. Francisca, *or throwing axe, from Howletts, Kent. London, British Museum*

manuscripts, which are often considerably longer than a man's height. A similar length is indicated also by the distance between the tip of the spearhead and the tip of the ferrule in graves at Chessel Down and Petersfinger.

Sword, *scramasax,* shield and spear – these are the com‚ monest weapons found in Anglo‚Saxon graves and on Anglo‚ Saxon sites. We must, however, deal with certain other armour which is found more rarely: the axe, the helmet, the bow and arrow, the angon and the coat of mail. A popular weapon of the pagan period on the continent was the *francisca* or throwing axe, which has a comparatively short handle and a head which curves upwards from the handle at a wide angle to a slightly upturned blade. This form is mainly Frankish but, although of rare occurrence, it is found in this country on one or two sites, mainly in Kent; one example, from Howletts, has an inlaid gilt plate on the head. A commoner type of axe in the later Saxon period is that which has a blade with a broad curved edge, mounted at right angles to the shaft; this was used as a battle‚axe in hand‚to‚hand fighting and it is seen put to this use in the Bayeux tapestry, by which time the battle‚axe is

Fig. 28

Fig. 26

a particularly English weapon (Stenton describes it as the traditional weapon of the house-carles) although it had not, as Miss Keller suggests, ousted the spear. This type of axe, with the curved and often drooping blade, was probably also used for chopping wood (although the T-shaped axe was particularly used for this purpose). Such axes as that from Sutton Hoo, which has a metal haft, must be a battle-axe; the iron haft could not be cut through by a well-directed blow from another axe – indeed it would turn the blade and provide an unpleasant shock for the person who dealt the blow.

Only three helmets have been found in Anglo-Saxon contexts. One from Leckhampton Hill, Gloucestershire, is now lost and a description and an engraving is all that survives. The helmet was formed of two crossed bronze bands joined at the top by an ornamental button and affixed at the bottom to a head band which had loops to which were attached, at either side, a chain. The second helmet was found at

Plate 29

Benty Grange in Derbyshire in 1848 and is a very elaborate object. The cap is made up of a framework of flat iron bands built up in a spherical form, with a nose guard decorated with the sign of the cross in silver. The gaps between the bands were originally filled in with horn plates (which no longer survive) attached by means of rivets with ornamental silver heads of

Plate 28

double-axe shape. The crest of the helmet is in the form of a boar, which is decorated with silver-gilt plates and studs, and its eyes are garnets set in filigree gold mounts. It has been suggested that the body of the boar was originally enamelled. The third helmet from an Anglo-Saxon grave is from Sutton Hoo: this is, in all probability, an imported piece and has been discussed elsewhere.

The presence of the boar, a Celtic symbol of some importance, on the Benty Grange helmet illuminates a number of passages in Anglo-Saxon literature, particularly a passage from *Beowulf*, where a helmet is personified as a boar:

On that pyre could be plainly seen
the bloody mail shirt and the golden swine,
The iron-hard boar . . .

The 'golden . . . iron-hard boar' must be related to the most conspicuous part of the Benty Grange helmet. It is interesting to note that a boar is depicted as the crest of a helmet on that exceptional first-century Celtic object, the Gundestrup cauldron.

The helmet was not a common piece of armour in the Saxon period – it seems to have been worn only by a chieftain or a rich man. On the Franks Casket, for instance, only the helmets of the leaders are depicted with neck guards and nose pieces; other warriors have soft leather (?) hats. Even on the Continent, in the contemporary Germanic graves, helmets are rare, although they occur in Germany and Sweden much more frequently than in England. In the manuscripts of the Christian period the helmet appears to be worn chiefly by those in authority. The type of helmet worn by the warrior, with its conical cap and nose guard, was evidently in common use among the cavalry at the battle of Hastings. Unfortunately no helmets of this type survive in this country, although comparable examples exist elsewhere, for example, the helmet of St Wenceslaus in Prague Cathedral, which, like the Benty Grange helmet has a Christian symbol (in this case the Crucifixion) on the nose guard. It seems probable that by the end of the Saxon period the helmet was a common piece of armour, as witness the reference in the *Anglo-Saxon Chronicle* for 1008 where every eight hides of land had to provide a helmet and a corselet. But Miss Keller is doubtless right when she says that the helmet was a comparatively rare piece of armour until this period. The ordinary soldier probably wore the so-called Phrygian cap, which may have been, as Laking suggests, lined with metal.

Archers are represented on the eighth-century Franks

Plate 56

121

Casket, on the Bayeux tapestry and on numerous manuscripts of the Anglo-Saxon period. Bows and arrows are, however, extremely rare in Anglo-Saxon graves. At Chessel Down, Hillier records that 'the presence of the bow, about five feet in length, could be distinctly traced by the dark line of decomposed wood in the chalk', and Baldwin-Brown records a similar feature at Bifrons. Also at Chessel Down were found arrowheads and traces of the shafts of a number of arrows, which the excavator presumed were made of the 'small straight wood of the hazel'. Arrowheads are sometimes found, but they are not a common Anglo-Saxon antiquity and Baldwin-Brown has pointed out that they may easily be confused with the head of a spear or a javelin; there appear to be both socketed and tanged arrowheads, some of which were certainly barbed, but one must presume that most arrows had no metal point and were merely hardened in the fire. At Oberflacht in Swabia for example a series of arrows was found, each some two feet in length, which were 'so withered that we took them for bowstrings', no arrowheads were attached to them and only a brownish colouring was seen where the points should have been. At this same site were found a number of bows, one of which was seven feet long. They were made of yew and were thickest in the centre, tapering towards the end and slightly curved. These bows must have been strong enough to deserve the description given to the bow in an Anglo-Saxon riddle:

WOB is my name reversed;
I am a strange creature, shaped amid combat.
When I bend, and the venomous dart
goes from my bosom, I am quite ready
to sweep that danger to life far from me.
When my master who thus tormented me
released my limbs, I am longer than before,
until, fraught with destruction, I spit out

the very deadly venom I had previously swallowed.
What I am speaking about does not
easily pass away from any man,
if what flies from my belly reaches him
so that he pays for the evil drink with his strength
and quickly makes full compensation with his life.
When I am unstrung I will not obey anyone
until I am skilfully tied. Say what I am.

The bow was the weapon of the foot soldier and of the common man and served for both the chase and for battle. The arrows were carried in a quiver, which was slung over the shoulder, and were flighted with feathers. The bows in the Bayeux tapestry appear to be about four feet in length but it would be unwise to make any judgment of size from contem-porary illustration alone. The only surviving early medieval bow from England is that from Berkhamsted Castle which may be of an early thirteenth-century date; like the bows on the tapestry it is about four feet in length, which agrees with most of the bows found at Oberflacht. It has been suggested that the bow was not a typical Anglo-Saxon weapon; perhaps there is some truth in this in the light of Henry of Huntingdon's record of William the Conqueror's reproach of the Saxons for their bad bowmanship.

Agathias, writing of the wars between Justinian and the Teutonic invaders of Italy, records that the chief weapon of the invaders was a light, barbed weapon which could be used as a javelin or in hand-to-hand fighting. 'The haft is covered with lamina so that little wood can be seen.' Agathias's description is a little confusing, and attempts to identify the weapon des-cribed have never been entirely satisfactory. It may be the angon, which is mainly found on the Continent, but which does occur in this country and especially in Kent, where it has been found at Sarre, Bifrons, High Down and Strood. Another example

Fig. 29. Transporting weapons, from the Bayeux Tapestry

comes from Beddington in Surrey. But these weapons are so undoubtedly foreign, and so rare of occurrence in the Anglo-Saxon area, that we need not discuss them here.

The coat of mail, which can be seen so frequently on the Bayeux tapestry, is a rare find in this country. Fragments of a mail-coat have been found at Sutton Hoo and the Benty Grange helmet was covered with mail when found. Nothing survives of the Benty Grange mail and it is possible that it was merely the neck guard of the helmet (a helmet with a mail neck guard occurred in the more or less contemporary grave 6 at Valsgärde in Sweden). The mail from the Sutton Hoo grave is corroded together, but undoubtedly formed a mail shirt. It differs from all the other surviving pre-Conquest chain-mail in Europe in that the links are not riveted, but merely butted together – a weak construction that had nothing to recommend it save ease of manufacture. The mail-shirts depicted in the Bayeux tapestry have short wide sleeves and

Figs. 29, 30

skirts which are divided in front and behind, for ease in riding. Sir James Mann has pointed out that these splits in the skirt must not be interpreted as an indication that the shirt was a garment which looked like a pair of combinations; the dis-comforts of riding in such a garment would have taxed the endurance of even the hardiest Viking. Such suits of mail must have been expensive to make and were obviously worn only by leaders and chieftains, a leather jerkin being sufficient protec-tion for the more humble members of society. The mail-shirt would itself be worn over a leather jerkin or even over a padded vest, so that the interlocking rings might not be driven into the flesh when pierced.

Fig. 30. Warrior, from the Bayeux Tapestry

In order to examine the method of warfare used by the Anglo-Saxons, I have taken a description of a battle and drawn from it conclusions as to the handling of weapons and the methods of fighting. On August 11th 991, near Maldon in Essex, was fought the battle which is known by the name of that town. It was fought on the banks of the River Blackwater; the Danes were initially on the Island of Northey and ulti- mately crossed, as a result of the Saxons' bad strategy, to the mainland by means of a causeway that is visible to this day. The battle was commemorated by a tapestry, which no longer exists, presented to the Abbey of Ely by the widow of Bryhtnoth, the English leader, and by the vernacular Anglo- Saxon poem which I have translated below. I have cut from the poem some of the rhetorical passages, which, though interesting, do not concern us here:

Then he ordered each soldier to dismount and drive his horse away from the field and to rely on his hand and his steadfastness. Then Bryhtnoth began to draw up his men; he rode and advised them, told them how they should stand and keep their ranks, and how they might best hold their shields firm with their hands. He encouraged them. When he had drawn up his army he dismounted among those people who pleased him most, where his retainers were most devoted. [At this point the Vikings send a messenger offering to refuse battle if the English will give them money; this offer is con- temptuously turned down.] Then he [Bryhtnoth] ordered the warriors, carrying their shields, to move forward until they all stood on the river bank. [After holding the causeway for a short time Bryhtnoth over-confidently allows the enemy to cross the ford.] Then the battle wolves, the Viking horde, were not hampered by the water. They came over the Black- water with their shields, westwards over the gleaming flood, the seamen with their linden shields. Bryhtnoth and his men stood there waiting for the enemy. He ordered them to form a wall with their shields and to stand firm against the foe. The fight, and the glory which comes with it, was now close to hand. The time was now come when the doomed should fall. All was clamour, ravens circled above, the eagle eager for carrion. There was a cry on the earth.

They let the file-hardened spears, the grim-ground javelins, fly from the hand. Bows were busy, point pierced shield, the rush of battle was fierce, warriors fell on all sides, the young men lay dead . . . Bryhtnoth's kinsman, his sister's son, was cruelly hewn down by swords . . . A man hardened in battle advanced to meet the warrior [i.e. Bryhtnoth] and raised his weapon, his shield as his defence. The earl, in no way less bold, advanced towards the 'churl', each bent on evil to the other. Then the Viking threw a southern spear, which wounded the lord of the warriors, who banged the spear with his shield so that the shaft broke; the spear was shivered and fell away from him. The warrior was angry and with his spear struck the proud Viking who had given him the wound. The warrior was skilful and ran his spear through the young warrior's neck; his hand guided it so that it killed the Viking.

Then he struck another raider so that his corselet burst and he was wounded in the breast through the chain mail; the fatal point reached his heart. [Bryhtnoth is again wounded.] A man then advanced on the earl to rob him of his warrior's trappings, the spoil and rings and ornamented sword.

Then Bryhtnoth drew his broad and brown-edged sword from his sheath and struck him on his corselet. Too quickly another Viking checked his hand, crippling the earl's arm. The yellow-hilted sword fell to the ground and he could not hold a sword or use a weapon. [After a heroic speech Bryhtnoth and his two retainers are killed, whereupon some warriors flee the field while others are rallied by heroic speeches and are gradually struck down.] Then, eagerly, the hostage helped them; he was called Aescferth and was the son of Ecglaf, and came from a good Northumbrian family. He did not draw away from the fight, but shot his arrows unceasingly, sometimes hitting a shield, sometimes a warrior. As long as he could wield his weapons, he dealt out wounds as much as he could.

Edward the Tall stood yet at the forefront of the battle. . . He broke the shield-wall and fought with the warriors until he had worthily taken vengeance on the seamen for the death of his chief and lay among the slain.

That noble retainer Aetheric, the brother of Sibirht, eager and impetuous, also fought boldly, as did many others; they hacked away the beaked shield and were valiant. The rim of the shield burst and the war-shirt sang a fearful song . . . Then were the shields broken: the Vikings advanced en-raged by the battle . . . Bryhtwold, an old retainer, spoke, raised aloft his shield, shook his ashen-spear and encouraged the warriors boldly. 'Purpose shall be harder, heart more valiant, courage greater as strength grows weaker. Here lies our lord, cut down, the noble man in the dust. He who thinks to turn now from the fight will long regret it. I am old. I will not flee but will lie by the side of my lord – that so much loved man.'

Nothing remains of the battle of Maldon except a cause-way in the Essex marshes and a letter recording the find of Bryhtnoth's skeleton in Ely Cathedral in 1769. The battle was not of extreme importance, it is dismissed by the *Anglo-Saxon Chronicle* in a few words. This poem, however, written not long after the battle while individual acts of valour were still fresh in the mind, enables us to reconstruct something of the art of war in the Anglo-Saxon period.

As was usual in Anglo-Saxon times the battle was fought on foot; only rarely are there references to cavalry engagements. Anglo-Saxon battles were fairly solid affairs: once the forces had met, the battle consisted of grim hand-to-hand fighting in a restricted area, the opposing sides hacking away at each other until one side was reduced to carrion or broke and fled. It is obvious from this poem that, despite the well-organized political structure of the period, the army was bound by the pagan heroic tradition based on the warrior's duty to his lord: when the chief was in the ascendant his companion or retainer enjoyed the glory and the spoils of victory; conversely, the retainer suffered with his chief, even, like Brythwold and Aetheric, dying by their chief's side. It was considered some-thing of a disgrace to flee from battle after the death of one's chief (although by the late Anglo-Saxon period even 'the right side' could flee with some impunity), and even a Christian like Asser cannot help letting a hint of criticism creep into his writings when the Saxons fled from the field after the death of a chief. As a consequence, battles were bloody and long drawn-out affairs.

By the very end of the Anglo-Saxon period the heroic battle was superseded by a more open fight on horseback and, at the battle of Stamford Bridge in 1066, there is some evidence that cavalry was used, if ineptly, by the Anglo-Saxons. Even so, the Anglo-Saxons fought the battle of Hastings largely on foot and one of the factors contributing to their defeat may have been their lack of mobility, although it has been very rightly pointed out that the Normans were not properly disciplined cavalry-men – they manœuvred rather as a body of mounted in-fantrymen.

From the Maldon poem it can be seen that the leader of the Anglo-Saxons took some care to draw up his men in line of battle. He was apparently at pains to create a wall of shields. It has been suggested that this shield-wall was in the nature of the Roman *testudo*, that, to use Professor Gordon's words, 'the shield-wall was a defensive formation made by ranks of men placed closely one behind another and holding their shields side by side and overlapping so as to present a continuous wall. The front rank of men held their shields before their breasts and the ranks behind held theirs over their heads to protect both those in front and themselves.' This interpretation must be basically true (*pace* Oman), but there is a certain formality about it which seems foreign to the idea of a Saxon battle. First of all I think we must discount the idea that the shields were interlocked; this would give no room to manœuvre, and even in the very formal construction of the Roman *testudo* the shields were not held so that they overlapped. Again, it is doubtful whether the men in the second rank, if indeed there were a second rank, would hold their shields over their own heads and the heads of those in the front rank; there would be too much risk of entanglement, one rank with another, in such a tight and solid formation. The first shock of battle was a hail of arrows and javelins from either side; it would be impossible to draw a bow or throw a javelin if the suggested formation were held. One can only believe that the army was ranged more or less in a line, with little space between each soldier, and that the shield was held in front of the body so that the head was protected, and at an angle to the body so that maximum protection was afforded to each man. This would give the impression to the opposing army of a wall composed of shields. Any second rank would hold the shield in the same way; when a warrior 'broke the shield-wall' he presumably fought his way through the line of shields.

The shield indeed played an important part in the battle: it took, or turned, arrows and javelins and sometimes became so weighed down with them that it had to be cast away; it acted as a defence in hand-to-hand fighting and, as in the poem quoted, was used to turn aside the spear thrust. We have many references in the literature to the orb being cut away and we must imagine that sometimes nothing was left in the hand but the boss which could then be used very effectively as a mailed fist – indeed there are references to the shield being used as a weapon of offence. After the battle it would be an easy matter to replace the broken orb.

The sword was used as a cutting weapon and the spear for thrusting, and the importance of these weapons is amply brought out in this poem which so well illuminates the art of war in the Anglo-Saxon period.

CHAPTER V
Anglo-Saxon Art

THE ORIGINS OF ANGLO-SAXON ART are threefold: insular Celtic, classical Mediterranean and continental Germanic. Each influenced the growth of the national art, and the importance of each varied through the years. Sir Thomas Kendrick has described the art of Anglo-Saxon England before 900 as 'a series of conflicts between the mutually irreconcilable principles of the barbaric and classical aesthetic systems'; but perhaps it would be better described as a struggle for reconciliation between the two systems, a reconciliation that was achieved twice: first in the early eighth century and then again in the tenth and eleventh centuries. The history of Anglo-Saxon art is extremely complex and, in the space at my disposal, I can only tackle it in a completely straightforward manner, showing simply its historical sequence and avoiding as many controversial elements as possible.

The clue to our understanding of Anglo-Saxon art lies in the fact that the barbaric artist abhorred naturalism as much as the classical artist of the Mediterranean abhorred the abstract. The Anglo-Saxon artist never attempted accurate portrayal of a human or animal form. He approached his subject in an abstract manner, breaking the surfaces and lines into a kaleidoscope of broken, twisted, tortuous and dismembered animal forms, which are completely divorced from the naturalism or his Mediterranean contemporary.

We must also bear in mind, in our discussion of the art of this people, the limited nature of the material that survives. For the first 250 years of the period under review our appreciation of the artistic achievement of the Anglo-Saxons is confined to the motifs which appear on jewellery and other similar articles of metal, stone or bone. There is no painting, no wood-carving or monumental art. From the last 350 years a considerable body of rather specialized painting and sculpture survives, which enables us to gain some idea of the richness of the art of this period; but the illuminated service books, Bibles, psalters and benedictionals which survive today do not tell us much about the wall paintings, stained glass windows and secular painting. Similarly, the memorial and preaching crosses, which are to be found in parish churches throughout the country, give no idea of the quality of the wood-carving and other plastic arts of the Anglo-Saxons. The surviving material, by its very nature, must give us a biased opinion of Anglo-Saxon art – our picture can never be complete, – but where there is a tendency to condemn and say, 'There is no art', we should remember that our evidence is slight and unreliable.

PAGAN METALWORK AND JEWELLERY

Generalizations are dangerous, but as far as the material allows us to make such a statement, pagan Anglo-Saxon art is based on two techniques, chip-carving and polychrome jewelling, and on two forms, animal ornament and abstract linear shapes. One of the techniques (chip-carving) and one of the forms (animal ornament) have their origin in the classical world, while the other two originate in the Celtic world of Britain and the rest of Europe. There can be little doubt that Celtic art had lost most of its momentum towards the end of the Roman period in Europe, and that the Celtic artists of Britain, of the Rhine and of the Danube were adapting, without any great vitality, the art of the Classical world. But a single spark, the chip-carving technique, seems to have kindled the Celtic-Germanic imagination to produce a new and exciting art. Chip-carving is a technique used originally in the carving of hard-wood and adapted by the Romans to metalwork. A running lozenge pattern of conjoined X's is marked out on the surface to be decorated; a corner of the chisel is then placed in the centre of the X and the material, wood or metal, is cut along the line of each leg so that the cut is deepest in the centre and just touches the surface at the end of the leg. The material, thus loosened by the chisel, is carved away so that, instead of an X marked on the surface, there is a pyramidal hole in its place. This technique, or a variant of it which produces a long V-shaped incision, is then used all over the surface

Plates, 30, 32   to give a glittering faceted effect. It was developed along the borders of the Rhenish Empire and spread from the Rhine to England. A group of buckle-plates, decorated in this manner and manufactured in the Rhenish area, is even found in this country. Such objects as these attracted the Anglo-Saxon aesthetic sense and were to influence the Anglo-Saxon metal-worker considerably. With the introduction of chip-carving the Germanic metal-worker also became interested in adapting non-geometrical motifs to this technique; experiments were made with spirals and leaves, and the rather weak Romano-Germanic animal ornament, with its slightly abstract and flaccid appearance, was tightened up into an animal style that

Plate 34   ultimately was to affect the whole of Europe. The Roman and Germanic background to this ornament is clearly seen in the decoration of the equal-armed brooch from Haslingfield, Cambridgeshire, which was probably manufactured in the Rhineland and brought into this country by one of the earliest settlers. The brooch has chip-carved scroll ornament and backward-looking animals lying along the internal borders.

A considerable proportion of the Anglo-Saxon metal-workers' art, during the next two or three centuries, was based on animals executed in the chip-carving technique. 'The

Fig. 31   creature', wrote Sir Thomas Kendrick, 'loses its zoological reality and is converted into mere pattern. Heads and legs, tails and teeth, are mixed together into an attractive pot-pourri of confusion which covers every square inch of the surface of the object.' This same decoration is encountered both in Germany

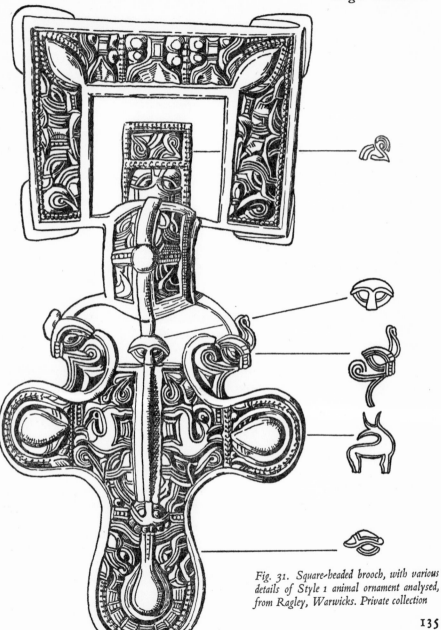

Fig. 31. *Square-headed brooch, with various details of Style 1 animal ornament analysed, from Ragley, Warwicks. Private collection*

135

and Scandinavia, as well as in Hungary and Eastern Europe, and it is not easy to decide where this animal style, of which the Anglo-Saxon style is but a phase, first appeared. There is a tendency to believe that the broad features of the Anglo-Saxon animal style originated in Scandinavia, but it is difficult to pin-point the priority of any particular piece. There can be little doubt, however, that the main features of early Anglo-Saxon art were introduced into England from the Continent and that, once introduced, they flourished in their own individual manner, at the same time influencing, and being influenced by, the Scandinavian and Germanic art.

The striking similarity between the English and Scandinavian material has often been illustrated: it was this similarity which made Bernhard Salin combine the Scandinavian and English animal ornament of the fifth and sixth centuries under the general classification, 'Style I'. The distinction at the time was good, but the term 'Style I', when applied to English animal ornament today, is misleading, for it lumps English ornament together with other ornament which has a distinctly different flavour. Sir Thomas Kendrick was the first person to attempt to break away from this label and from the label 'Style II' which Salin had given to the more sinuous ribbon-like treatment of animal ornament that was introduced into this country towards the end of the pagan period. The first style was called by Kendrick the 'Helmet and Hand Style', and the second the 'Ribbon Style'; the second title is ideal, but the first gives no impression of the style it describes and archae-ologists are forced to use the old classification of Salin.

The restless movement of the first animal style with its broken lines and abstract forms was replaced by a quieter, apparently simpler, ornament based on the interlacing and interplay of the ribbon-like bodies of animals and snakes. In effect the new art of the Ribbon Style was not very far in its aims from the earlier disjointed art of the first style. The aim was still to cover the ornamented surface with complicated animal and tendril ornament. There was still no tendency to realism. Symmetry was used or ignored at will; on the Crundale Down sword *Fig. 32, right* pommel symmetry is very strictly adhered to; on the great gold buckle from Sutton Hoo, the structure of the buckle is sym- *Fig. 32, left* metrical, but only the heads of the animals are placed symmetrically – their bodies wander off into tight, pleasing knots and into loose skilful loops all over the surface of the object. The origins of the Ribbon Style are obscure, but ultimately it is based on Romano-Germanic ornament. Some say that it originated in Scandinavia, others, in Italy. The discussion is yet to be resolved.

Fig. 32. Ribbon-style animal ornament, from the Sutton Hoo buckle and from a sword pommel from Crundale Down. London, British Museum

In this country there is an interesting fusion between the two styles, which is seen at its best on parts of the Taplow horn mounts – disjointed ornament of the first style is combined with the interlaced ornament of the Ribbon Style. (Incidentally, it is interesting to note that both Style I and the Ribbon Style, as well as the Fusion Style, all occur on different parts of the Taplow drinking-horn.) It seems likely that the Ribbon Style is a seventh-century phenomenon, while the first style belongs to the fifth and sixth centuries. An interesting feature of the Ribbon Style, and one that can be seen on the clasp and buckle from Taplow, is the combination of a false chip-carved effect *Plate 44* with filigree wire. The false chip-carved effect is achieved by pressing gold and silver sheets into pitch, to produce a pattern similar to chip-carving, and capping the lines that stand up in relief with beaded wire.

One of the most important and striking elements in the art of the Anglo-Saxon pagan period is the rich polychrome jewellery of Kent and East Anglia. The whole story of poly-chrome jewellery is bedevilled by a controversy which was started in the 1930's by Sir Thomas Kendrick, and which has not yet been resolved in print. Although specialists are quite happy in their own minds that Sir Thomas Kendrick's theories have been proved wrong, his theory has stood un-challenged for twenty years. Mr Jessup's useful discussion of the Anglo-Saxon jewellery, which is the only work that has been published on the subject since Kendrick's book, avoided chronological judgments, and the only really convincing arguments against Kendrick's theory were given orally by Mr Bruce-Mitford in a lecture to the Society of Antiquaries in 1954. In his lecture Mr Bruce-Mitford demolished in a detailed manner the whole structure of Kendrick's arguments and the broad lines of Mr Bruce-Mitford's thesis were not challenged. Basically, Kendrick pleaded 'for a central date about A.D. 500 as an indicator of the period when most (not all) of the jewels were being worn'. Since Kendrick wrote these words the great Sutton Hoo treasure has been found and the large number of pieces (thirty-four in all) of polychrome jewellery found there have been conclusively proved to have been deposited between 650 and 660. In the face of this and other evidence which has entailed the re-dating of such objects as the Cross of St Cuthbert, most Anglo-Saxon archaeologists would agree that the English polychrome jewellery flourished in the period 550–700.

Polychrome jewellery is so called because it is inlaid with garnets, blue and green glass, niello and white shell. There are two types of polychrome jewellery. The first is a rich, luxurious jewellery in which flat-cut stones and glass are set in gold or silver cells, built up from bands of metal on a base plate of gold or silver. (These cells give the polychrome jewellery another name, cloisonné, from the French *cloison* – a cell.) Another feature of this group of jewellery is the use of panels of filigree-wire ornament which are spaced between the cells: similarly the same wire is often used to build up a border for the jewel. The most luxurious example of this class is the Kingston brooch.

Plate 35

The second class of polychrome jewellery is much humbler; the base plate and cells are cast in one piece, as is the incidental ornament, which sometimes has a serrated edge in imitation of the filigree technique. These cells are filled with garnets; coloured glass rarely occurs. The borders of many of the objects in this class are decorated with small black rings of niello. One of the features, which occurs very rarely in the humbler class of polychrome jewellery but which is often found in the richer group, is the small punched sheets of gold foil which are placed at the bottom of each cell behind the garnet. These sheets, punched in various patterns, abound in the Sutton Hoo jewellery, for instance, and serve to reflect the light back through the garnet at different angles, thus giving a sparkling and lively effect to a stone which would otherwise be rather dull and flat. Some of the empty cells in the Wilton cross have lost their garnets but retained their foil.

Plates, 36, 37

Plate 42

The objects most commonly executed in the polychrome manner are disc brooches which are most frequently found in Kent, but the technique in its application to other objects is well documented; garnets, for example, quite frequently embellish the great square-headed brooches. There are, however, two distinct areas of manufacture of Anglo-Saxon polychrome jewellery – Suffolk and Kent. The Suffolk, or East Anglian, school, which is typified by the jewellery found at Sutton Hoo, can be distinguished from the Kentish material

Plate 42

{ Plate 1
{ *Fig. 3*

Plate 39

by the shapes of the individual garnets. Many of the Sutton Hoo and East Anglian garnets are cut to the shape of a mushroom (to be seen, for example, on the arms of the Wilton Cross where they join the central circle); others are curved to make animal patterns, boar's heads, etc., as on the epaulettes and the purse lid from the Sutton Hoo burial. Nowhere else in Europe at this period are such large pieces of garnet used in the design of polychrome jewellery. The Kentish school is typified by the disc brooches with their simpler cell patterns.

The shapes of the cells in the richer class of polychrome jewellery have been the basis for considerable discussion as to the origin of the technique. Most of the features of the Anglo-Saxon polychrome jewellery occur abroad in Italy, Sweden or the Low Countries. Although, generally speaking, the English material is of the highest quality, it would be extremely difficult to decide whether, for instance, the Wynaldum buckle-plate, found recently in Holland was made by a Dutch or an English craftsman or whether, in the words of Mr Bruce-Mitford, it was perhaps 'the work of a craftsman trained in Kent or Suffolk but working for a Continental patron'. Polychrome jewellery has its roots in two cultures, the Romano-Celtic Culture, with its interest in polychrome brooches and other ornaments worked in enamel, and in the Gothic Culture of the Black Sea area, where the craftsmen had perhaps inherited some of the techniques and skill of the Scythians. The great fourth-century treasure of Petrossa, Roumania, and the Szilagy-Somlyo treasure from Hungary demonstrate the richness of the cloisonné technique in Eastern Europe, while, nearer home, the rich treasure (buried in 481) from Childeric's tomb found at Tournai, Belgium, gives us some idea of the high quality of the polychrome technique in Western Europe. Closer study of the polychrome technique in Continental Europe may ultimately reveal its origins; meanwhile, all that can be said is that in England the technique reached heights unexcelled elsewhere.

Lastly, in our discussion of the art of the Anglo-Saxon pagan period, we must consider certain Celtic influences and motifs. These Celtic motifs occur most commonly on the fairly large group of objects known as hanging-bowls. The bowls are all, with two late exceptions, made of bronze and vary in diameter between about eight inches and eighteen inches; they have at the rim three rings for suspension, clasped to the bowl by means of hooks which develop from an ornamental plaque or escutcheon. In later examples the escutcheons are often enamelled and another escutcheon is attached inside the bowl on the bottom. These escutcheons are decorated in a curvilinear spiral style which has its roots in the native British Celtic ornament. The question of the hanging-bowl has already been discussed in relation to Sutton Hoo (p. 47 f.). The bowls, however, are but one aspect of this revival of interest in Celtic forms and shapes. The boar, which acts as a crest on the Benty Grange helmet, is in a direct line of descent from the large number of boars portrayed in a similar form by the pre-Roman Celts – boars are also depicted on the sword from the river Lark, which we have already mentioned, and on the Sutton Hoo epaulettes. In the field of human portraiture there are also some interesting Celtic connections. The heads carved on the Sutton Hoo and Hough-on-the-Hill whetstones, for example, have surely some Celtic connection and may have reached Anglo-Saxon art either through Scotland or Ireland. This Celtic repertoire passes full-bloodedly into Anglo-Saxon art. In the late seventh and eighth centuries we see these motifs used in the manuscripts, as well as on metal and bone objects. The developed spiral patterns, which appear in such a skilfully executed form in the Lindisfarne Gospels (implicitly dated by inscription to about 700), are but developments of the orna-mental motifs appearing on the Middleton Moor escutcheon. An ivory box of English manufacture from Gandersheim (now in the Ducal Museum, Brunswick) has an animal style which

Plates 43, 45

Plates 28, 29

Plate 10

Plate 48

Plate 43
Fig. 7

is presumably of eighth-century date; in the middle of the bottom of one side is a panel completely taken up by a developed spiral motif – one of its last definite occurrences in Anglo-Saxon art.

THE EFFECT OF CHRISTIANITY

All the art which we have discussed so far has been, with one or two exceptions, applied art, ornament on metal brooches and other objects of utility. The church was to introduce into this country a completely new art form, painting, and was to rekindle a dormant interest in monumental sculpture. These forms of art were not immediately adopted, just as Christianity was not immediately adopted. No manuscripts written in England before the last half of the seventh century are known to survive and a similar statement could probably be made about Anglo-Saxon sculpture, if we had but a single piece of firm dating evidence for this particular art form in this early period.

METALWORK: SEVENTH TO NINTH CENTURIES

It is often difficult for the professional archaeologist to remember that the Sutton Hoo cenotaph, essentially such a pagan phenomenon, was laid down more than half a century after the Augustinian mission, and that most of the jewellery found at Sutton Hoo, and indeed most of the metalwork ornamented in the Ribbon Style, was probably made after the official introduction of Christianity into this country. It must be stressed that the introduction of Christianity did not put an end to the work of the pagan Anglo-Saxon jeweller. We have seen how he adapted his craft to making such Christian objects as the pectoral cross of St Cuthbert and the other associated crosses. The metalworker merely changed his religion because he considered it politic and continued to work in the tradition of his masters and his forefathers, developing his art and broadening his repertoire. Naturally he was influenced by the newly

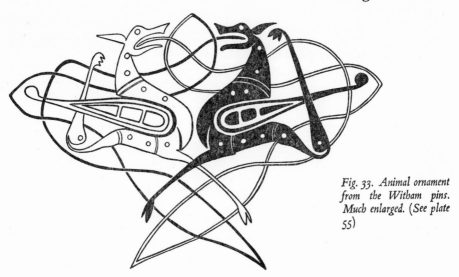

Fig. 33. Animal ornament from the Witham pins. Much enlarged. (See plate 55)

introduced arts, but he continued to work with the familiar forms. The last fling of the polychrome jeweller's use of garnet is to be seen in the garnets he placed at the terminals of the trefoil brooch found in the Kirkoswald hoard (dated 855). But the strength of the chip-carving tradition is to be seen on the Witham pins, where the glittering gilt bronze emphasizes the animals, skilfully interlaced in a new and more naturalistic development of the Ribbon Style. It should not be thought that animals were the only motif used by the Anglo-Saxon artist of this period; scroll patterns are to be seen, for instance, on the Kirkoswald brooch and the use of foliage motifs is particularly marked. Occasionally the animals degenerated into foliage, as for example on the ring found a few years ago at Poslingford in Suffolk.

Chip-carved gilt bronze, as a technique, was replaced, towards the end of the ninth century by carved silver, sometimes inlaid with black niello or gold plates; the animals and other ornamental motifs were defined by shallow carving and

Plate 62

Plate 55
Fig. 33

Fig. 34

Plate 64

Fig. 34. Extended drawing of the ornament on the gold ring from Poslingford, Suffolk. London, British Museum

speckled all over with the corner of an engraving tool. The designs were, of course, marked out on the metal before being carved and these lines of construction can be seen on a number of objects. Sometimes the artist would try out his patterns and his animals on a piece of bone, as for example that found in the last century in York, before carving them in silver. This use of silver, resulting from the particular scarcity of gold at this period, has given the title of the 'silver age' to this phase of Anglo-Saxon art. Among the best examples of this style of silver work are certain mounts from a hoard from Trewhiddle in Cornwall, which has given its name to the style.

Plate 67

Plate 63
Fig. 35

The skill of the Anglo-Saxon metalworker of the Christian period was renowned throughout Europe. In Rome, Anglo-Saxon craftsmen of the *Schola Saxonum* were making vessels for the altar of St Peter's itself. When Duke Tassilo of Austria founded the monastery of Kremsmünster in the year 777, he gave to the abbey at least one piece of plate, a chalice, which bears his name, and which was almost certainly made by a craftsman trained in England or in the *Schola Saxonum* in Rome. The glittering gilt chip-carved surface of this object bears charming interlaced animals and foliate motifs of English origin, as well as portraits of Christ and the Apostles which are of Mediterranean influence; the animal ornament cannot be exactly paralleled in this country, but its style is so close to that of England that it must be seen as an Anglo-Continental style. The English styles also influenced the Irish and Scottish metalworker, then at the height of his powers. The animal patterns of the Kells crozier, for example, are extremely close to those of

Plate 61

Fig. 36

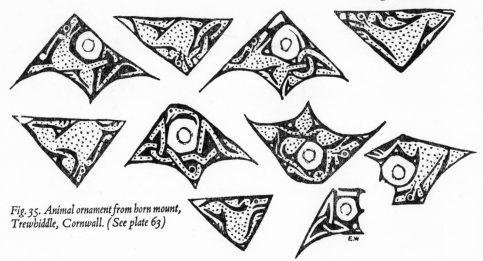

Fig. 35. *Animal ornament from horn mount,*
Trewhiddle, Cornwall. (See plate 63)

the Trewhiddle hoard, while some of the animal ornament on the newly found St Ninian's hoard is derived from the rather earlier Anglo-Saxon animal ornament, best seen in manu-script in the Lindisfarne Gospels. This style was not then cut off from the main-stream of European art: it was a style right in the centre of the stream. Its highest achievements are seen in such objects as the Fuller brooch, which is fine enough to stand beside any of the world's great jewellery. The ninth century was one of the greatest periods in the art of the Anglo-Saxon metal-worker: his command of his medium is well illustrated by the sword pommel from Fetter Lane in the City of London with its niello and parcel-gilt animal and leaf pattern, or by the object made at the command of King Alfred – the Alfred Jewel, one of the chief treasures of the University of Oxford.

Plate 65

Plate 24

Plates 57, 58

The Alfred Jewel, now in the Ashmolean Museum, which was found in 1693 in Newton Park, near the Island of Athelney in Somerset, is of gold with a crystal plaque covering the enamelled figure of a man holding two sceptres. The terminal takes the form of an animal's head and an Anglo-

Fig. 36. German, Irish and English animal ornament compared: (a) from the Tassilo Chalice; (b) the Kells crozier and (c) Trewhiddle horn mount

Saxon inscription round the edge reads, +AELFRED MEC HEHT GEWYRCAN (Alfred ordered me to be made). The back-plate is engraved with an elaborate foliate design which has Carolingian as well as Anglo-Saxon affinities. The animal-head terminal, which is executed in filigree wire and in granules of gold, must originally have been riveted to a wooden or ivory handle or staff. The use of the jewel is not known; its only parallel, apparently, is the Minster Lovell jewel, which is also preserved in the Ashmolean Museum at Oxford. These jewels are two of the rare examples from the late Saxon period of the technique of cloisonné enamel: another English example is the circular brooch from Dowgate Hill, with it representation of a nimbed or crowned figure, which is very close in style to the portrait in the Alfred Jewel.

Plate 59

Plate 60

MANUSCRIPTS: SEVENTH TO NINTH CENTURIES

At the end of the ninth century new motifs make themselves felt in the art of the metalworker, but for the moment we must retrace our steps and consider the other art forms practised by the Christian Anglo-Saxons. The Church brought to the pagan English the skill of writing and illuminating books. The illuminators had three sources for their art. From Mediter-ranean illumination the Anglo-Saxons borrowed the idea of naturalistic representation of the human figure, and certain other formulae of illumination, as, for example, the use of arcading to contain the canon tables (a concordance of references to corresponding passages in the different Gospels). From Ireland and the Celtic world probably came such features as the elaborate initials, particularly that which occurs in the 18th verse of Chapter I of St Matthew's Gospel, *Christi autem generatio sic erat* ('Now the birth of Christ was on this wise'). From the native Anglo-Saxon art came the use of elaborate ribbon interlace and animal ornament, together with the idea of covering whole pages with ornament to produce the so-called 'carpet pages'. There are, of course, many nuances within this rather simplified scheme of origins, and as the ancient barbaric spirit of the Anglo-Saxon gained the upper hand, so the direct Mediterranean influences became more obscure in the art of the scribe and the three influences fused into one characteristic Anglo-Saxon style.

The earliest surviving illuminated manuscript of Anglo-Saxon origin is the Book of Durrow (now in the Library of Trinity College, Dublin) which, although once thought to be of Irish origin, is now accepted by many scholars as a Northumbrian work. It dates from the last half of the seventh century and was probably written within a few years of 675. The purely decorative ornament of this book is completely in keeping with the insular ornament of the Ribbon Style and with such Celtic features as spiral scroll patterns of a form found on the hanging-bowl escutcheons. The symbols of the Evangelists, which act as a frontispiece to each gospel, make no concession to naturalism at all and are far removed from their Mediterranean prototypes, yet they are drawn with remarkable clarity. Similarity of style between certain motifs from the Book of Durrow and the enamelled hanging-bowl escutcheons is surely significant where the colour of the book is concerned. The reds and yellows of this book are the colours of the more or less contemporary enamels, and more direct

Plate 46

parallels to enamelling are to be seen on the figure of one of the evangelist symbols, whose robe is decorated with a pattern which imitates millefiori work. It has been suggested that some of the ornament of the Book of Durrow has its background in the Sutton Hoo treasure. The great decorative pages of Durrow have been compared with the rectangular panels of the Sutton Hoo shoulder clasps, and parallels drawn between the animal ornament of Durrow and that of Sutton Hoo. One of the new decorative elements, plain ribbon interlace, which first appears in the Book of Durrow, is in effect a regularized version of the earlier Ribbon Style without its zoomorphic characteristics. The Book of Durrow initiates one of the greatest periods of Anglo-Saxon art.

Plates 47–50
Written and illuminated in Northumbria, shortly after the Book of Durrow, is a small group of manuscripts of which the three most important are the Codex Amiatinus, the Lindis- farne Gospels and the Echternach Gospels. They were all produced within a few years of the turn of the seventh century. Two of these books, the Lindisfarne Gospels and the Echter- nach Gospels, continue in the insular tradition of the Book of Durrow, bringing it, however, to a perfection never before

Plate 47
attained. The third book, known as the Codex Amiatinus (now in the Laurentian Library at Florence) was one of the three copies of the Gospels (*'tres pandectes novae translationis',* as Bede describes them) written at the command of the first Abbot of Jarrow (Ceolfrith, died 716), one for the monastery of Monkwearmouth, one for the monastery of Jarrow and one for the Pope. This large and splendid book was the one destined for the Pope. Ceolfrith himself set out to deliver it in person, but on the way he died at Langres in France and the book had to be taken to Rome by his followers. The book was apparently modelled on one of those brought from Italy by Benedict Biscop and is entirely Italianate in the character of its illumina- tion. It is influenced only in a very minor way by the artistic

traditions of Northumbria, which is rather surprising when one considers that, at the same time as the Codex Amiatinus was made, only a few miles away on a small island off the coast of Northumberland, the Lindisfarne Gospels were being written and illuminated in a markedly Anglo-Saxon style by Eadfrith (Bishop of Lindisfarne 698–721). Recent studies have suggested that it was written and illuminated within a year or two of 698. This book, which is probably one of the finest works of art ever produced in England, synthesizes in its many illuminated pages the artistic traditions of three worlds, the Mediterranean, the Celtic North and Anglo-Saxon England. The four portraits of the Evangelists, for example, are based on Italian prototypes tautened by the economy of line of the insular scribe. The controlled exuberance of the interlaced animals in the carpet pages, with the jewel-like quality of their painting, is purely Anglo-Saxon. The animals are similar in certain respects to those on the Witham pins which, although much simpler, glitter in a manner that may be compared to the glow attained by the illuminator. The third of this group of manuscripts, the Echternach Gospels, which bears a cousinly relationship to the Lindisfarne Gospels without being quite so grand, was painted in Northumbria, probably (according to Mr Julian Brown) in the same scriptorum as the Lindisfarne Gospels, and was sent shortly afterwards to the newly founded German monastery of Echternach, where it became a model for a style of illumination which grew up there and which had its roots in Northumbria.

These great painted manuscripts of the late seventh and early eighth centuries obscure, with their brilliance, their more humble successors of the period between 725 and 850. Certain manuscripts, such as the Book of Chad in the Library of Lichfield Cathedral, continue the native Anglo-Saxon tradition of Durrow and Echternach, just as the great school of manuscripts painted, probably at Canterbury, between the

Plates 48, 49

Plate 55

Plate 51

Plate 52

middle of the eighth and the middle of the ninth century, retain many of the traits of the Lindisfarne group, while gradually taking into their ornamental repertoire the Continental motifs and ornaments of the Carolingian Renaissance. Two of the richest of these manuscripts are the Codex Aureus of the Royal Library in Stockholm and a Gospel book in the British Museum (Royal 1.E.VI). The great pages of purple vellum in these manuscripts give an impression of luxury and richness which is marred, in the case of Royal 1.E.VI at least, by the fact that the silver lettering has oxidized and obscured the brilliance of the painting. The portraits of the Evangelists and the frames round them in this Gospel book can be compared with those of such Carolingian manuscripts as the Godescalc Evangeliar, while the canon tables retain much of the incidental detail that was used in the Lindisfarne Gospels. However, in one of the earlier manuscripts of the school, the Canterbury Psalter in the British Museum, the frame which surrounds the portrait of David is of a completely Celtic character. The arch under which he sits, surrounded by his musicians, is composed of spirals of the type found on the hanging-bowls, while the columns which support the arch have an interlace ornament not unlike that of the Lindisfarne Gospels. This same Psalter and the Stockholm Codex Aureus have many minor illuminated initials, including, in the case of the former, initials which contain scenes illustrating Biblical happenings, a feature which occurs here for the first time and which was to be persistently popular throughout English medieval illumination. It is interesting, incidentally, to note that the richest and latest of this group of manuscripts, Royal 1.E.VI, contains no illuminated initials. Even in these books the metalworker's techniques are seen to be carried into the manuscript art: small speckled animals are reserved against a black background in a manner which imitates the silver and niello art of the Trewhiddle style. The Canterbury School succeeded the

Northumbrian School as the centre of English painting because of the difficult and troublous political situation in the north; it, in turn, was to be eclipsed in very much the same way by the Viking incursions into England. King Alfred's lamentations concerning the fall in the standard of learning in England, with which he prefaced his translation of Gregory's *Cura Pastoralis,* are reflected in the lack of late ninth-century manuscripts illuminated and written in England.

SCULPTURE: SEVENTH TO NINTH CENTURIES

The development of manuscript art in England was paralleled, on a lesser plane, by monumental sculpture. Of this group of monuments Sir Thomas Kendrick, writing in 1938, said: 'No department of our national antiquities is more urgently in need of organized study than the English crosses . . . it [is] an excessively embarrassing fact that the principal problems of chronology and stylistic development are not likely to be solved before a complete survey of the material has been accom-plished.' In 1960 every word of this trenchant remark is still true. The survey initiated by Kendrick has never been com-pleted and, although a lot of work is being done on this subject, we can expect no published survey for at least ten years. Any chronological judgments must be made purely statistically – an extremely dangerous thing to do. Here I can draw only the broad outlines of a hazy subject.

It seems probable that the idea of the Anglo-Saxon cross was developed on Celtic soil in Scotland, Wales and Ireland, and that it was one of the many innovations introduced into England with Christianity; in its turn, the Celtic cross or memorial stone was probably derived from a Romano-British prototype. The ornament of the earliest Anglo-Saxon sculp-ture, however, is derived from Mediterranean and Anglo-Saxon sources and rarely from Celtic sources. Both Professor Kitzinger and Sir Thomas Kendrick have pointed out that practically none of this ornament has any immediate Continental source, and even the assiduous work of Professor Brøndsted in investigating its origins had few concrete results. In the present context, then, it is best to ignore the vexed question of the origins of this monumental art and treat it as the individual insular phenomenon it is.

The most accomplished school of Anglo-Saxon carving in the seventh and eighth centuries appears to have been Northumbrian. Indeed the quality of the carving can broadly be said to follow the geographical trends of manuscript illumination: for towards the end of the eighth century Mercia and Southern England appear to have produced the greater works of art, so much so that, when in the early tenth century there was a revival of stone carving in the north, the first products were crude and ham-fisted in the extreme. The assembled corpus of Anglo-Saxon sculpture is so large that it is impossible to do justice to it in the space at my disposal. I intend therefore to describe certain pieces of exceptional quality and discuss them in their general context.

Plate 53

By far the most remarkable piece of Northumbrian sculpture is the eighteen-foot cross from Ruthwell in Dumfriesshire, which has been mentioned in an earlier chapter (p. 61); it should probably be thought of in the same chronological context as the Lindisfarne and Echternach Gospels. The four arms of the cross originally bore portraits of the four Evangelists but, unfortunately, only two arms survive. Below the head of the cross, on each of the broader faces of the shaft, are various Christian scenes: John the Baptist, Our Lord in Majesty, Paul and Anthony in the desert, the Flight into Egypt, the Visitation, Mary Magdalene washing Christ's feet, the Annunciation and the Crucifixion. The sides of the shaft bear an elaborate vine-scroll peopled with animals and birds, the whole motif known technically as an 'inhabited vine-scroll'. The scenes on the two faces and the panels on the sides of the cross are surrounded by plain borders, those on the sides bearing a rendering in runic lettering of one of the most beautiful of all the Anglo-Saxon poems, *The Dream of the Rood*. The borders of the pictorial panels bear Latin inscriptions describing the scenes depicted. The figure-carving on this cross was done by an artist who was more than usually competent in his medium: the carvings are deep, soft and full, and the features are portrayed with a naturalism rarely found in an Anglo-Saxon artist's work; yet that this was carved by an Anglo-Saxon sculptor cannot be doubted. There is a stiffness present that no Mediterranean-trained artist would have allowed. Kendrick has pointed out the awkwardness of the Mary Magdalene scene where the woman is so contorted as to be almost gross, while the drapery lacks the flow of any Mediterranean counterpart. Nearly every other example of Northumbrian sculpture, however, is more clumsy or less naturalistic than the Ruthwell cross. The Bewcastle cross, for instance, which may well have been modelled on the Ruthwell cross, has, in its portrayal of the human figures, more abstract or insular characteristics than the other possesses. Although similar panels of Biblical scenes are very popular in Northumbrian crosses, in many cases they become secondary to panels which contain abstract designs of interlaced animals and vine scrolls, 'inhabited' or otherwise.

Southern English art at the end of the eighth century was very much under the influence of the style of ornament typified in the Trewhiddle hoard and in the manuscript Royal 1.E.VI. Traces of sculpture in Southern England belonging to an earlier period are apparently rare, although the one important exception of the Reculver cross fragments must be mentioned. There is a reasonable possibility that these few miserable fragments are all that survive of a magnificent cross of seventh-century date: archaeological evidence, based on excavation, seems to support this theory. The fragments themselves show the cross to have been round-shafted, bearing figural scenes

Plates 52, 63

Fig. 35

which were surrounded in part by ribbon interlace. There is a delicacy about the carving that is not met with elsewhere in Anglo-Saxon sculptural art, but the pieces are unfortunately too fragmentary to be placed definitely in any context. For the rest, such Anglo-Saxon carving as is found in Mercia and southern England is very much influenced by the Northumbrian styles and by the art of the manuscripts. The cross-head

Plate 66

from Cropthorne, Worcestershire, for example, bears an animal which is closely related to the ones in the manuscript Royal 1.E.VI, while at the same time the birds and foliate ornament are direct descendants of the Northumbrian inhabited vine-scroll. The Cropthorne cross-head is one of the higher achievements of Southern Anglo-Saxon sculptural art of the ninth century, most of the surviving sculpture of this period and area being flat and undistinguished; it is not until the tenth century that the sculpture of Wessex and the south rises to its greatest heights.

It would not be fitting to leave the subject of Anglo-Saxon sculpture without some reference to two examples of Northumbrian carving which stand by themselves, removed from the

Plate 54

art of the monumental sculptor. The first is the oak coffin of St Cuthbert which was apparently made in 698. It is carved with linear representations of the Evangelists, the Apostles, the Archangels, etc., in a style similar to the Evangelist portraits in the Lindisfarne Gospels. Professor Kitzinger has shown that the figures have their stylistic origin on the Continent, in the same way that the Evangelist figures in the Echternach/Lindisfarne group have Continental connections, and that they are best paralleled in this country on the Ruthwell cross. The

Plate 56

second piece of Northumbrian carving which must be mentioned is the Franks Casket (so called after Sir Augustus Franks, Keeper of the Department of British Antiquities in the British Museum 1866–96, who gave it to the museum). It is of whalebone and is carved with scenes, taken from a universal history, of such diverse subjects as Wayland the Smith, the Capture of Jerusalem by Titus and the Adoration of the Magi. The whole of the box, each side of which is framed by a runic inscription, is carved with a barbaric abandon which is far removed from the slightly barbarized classicism of the Lindisfarne Evangelist portraits, the figures of the Ruthwell cross and the carvings of St Cuthbert's coffin. The casket stands by itself as an expression of the vernacular art of the early eighth century. These two pieces are important in so far as they are two of the very few objects which survive in such perishable materials, and serve to remind us that our knowledge of Anglo~ Saxon art is very one~sided.

THE TENTH~CENTURY RENAISSANCE

After Alfred's Viking wars came a period of political consoli~ dation which involved a series of campaigns against the Vikings, and it is with the accession of Edgar in 959 and with the monastic reforms of Oswald, Dunstan and Aethelwold, that England, and with it English art, achieved another period of greatness. Indeed, it might be possible to think of the late ninth and early tenth centuries as a period barren of artistic merit, if it were not for two objects: the stole and maniple found in the coffin of St Cuthbert.

Plate 68

Very little is known about English embroidery in the Anglo~ Saxon period, but literary references indicate its high quality. It is recorded, for example, that when William the Conqueror returned from a visit to England in the middle of the eleventh century, his Norman subjects were astonished by the quality of the robes he had acquired in England. Later, in the twelfth century, embroideries of 'English work' (*opus anglicanum*) were to become famous throughout Europe. Inscriptions on the stole and maniple of St Cuthbert imply that they were made, probably at Winchester, between 909 and 916. The figural subjects embroidered on them have already been described

(p. 64). The elongated figures are executed with remarkable sensitivity; they wear loosely draped clothes, their stance is well balanced and naturalistic, and their faces are by no means stereotyped. The figures are separated from each other by stiff, formal acanthus leaves. They are embroidered in blues, greens, pinks and browns and set against a golden background: the whole effect is one of extreme richness. The only other surviving English embroidery of this period is a fragment in the Basilica Ambrosiana in Milan.

These pieces demonstrate that, in the south of England at least, the sophisticated classes were turning to the Continent for artistic inspiration. The style of the stole and maniple of St Cuthbert is completely Carolingian and its ultimate origin is Byzantine: there is no trace of any insular stylistic trends. The poverty-stricken state of English art before the middle of the tenth century is reflected in all its forms, except only these few embroideries which are so Carolingian in their conception. In metalwork and sculpture the artist was struggling to attain the brilliance of his insular predecessors in the face of an influx of Scandinavian taste; and in the field of manuscript illumination the artist attempted to keep alive the English ninth-century art while trying, at the same time, to adopt Continental models. The fleshy Carolingian acanthus leaf and the decorated initials with their native Anglo-Saxon traditions do achieve competence, but never brilliance, in such manuscripts as the Junius Psalter (the Bodleian Library, Oxford) and, from Durham, the Life of St Cuthbert (Corpus Christi College, Cambridge).

MANUSCRIPTS FROM EDGAR TO THE CONQUEST

In the middle of the tenth century, however, a brilliant style of manuscript illumination of the highest quality was introduced, based on the Continental models which people like Dunstan had got to know during their visits, enforced or otherwise, to

France. These manuscripts are said to belong to the 'Winchester School', but it is important to realize that other places
besides Winchester had *scriptoria* which were every bit as
competent. The first surviving product of the new style is a
copy of the charter granted to the New Minster at Winchester
by King Edgar in 966, and which must date from the last half
of the tenth century. The text is written in letters of gold and
there are three ornamental pages, as well as the principal
illuminated page (on purple vellum) which shows the King
between the Virgin and St Peter offering the Charter to Christ
who sits in a mandorla supported by four angels. The figures
are well proportioned and their clothes are drawn with incisive
freedom. The faces of the figures are rather coarse, but this is
offset by their grace and sense of movement. An important
feature of this page is the formal border, consisting of a double
plain band-like frame entwined by a heavy and formal acanthus
ornament, which seems at odds with the lively quality of the
figures it encloses.

Plate 70

An even heavier border encloses the portraits and scenes in
the richest of all late Anglo-Saxon manuscripts, the Benedictional of St Aethelwold, now in the British Museum. The
borders were so important that they are mentioned in the
dedicatory inscription, and Professor Kitzinger has rightly
pointed out that each page should be seen, not as a portrait but
as 'a large and sumptuous openwork ornament'. We see here
the Anglo-Saxon artist's inherent attraction to ornament for
the sake of ornament that was so noticeable a feature of the
earlier manuscripts. Although the borders dominate the manuscript, they do not overbalance the constructional equilibrium.
The artist achieved here a high vitality in his human portraiture;
the scene of the Annunciation, for instance, shows an angel
amidst swirling draperies, in a naturalistic stance, drawn with
confidence and lightness. The faces have lost the coarseness of
those in the New Minster Charter, but there is perhaps a

Plate 69

stereotyped quality about them. The colouring of the manuscript is highly extravagant, pastel shades are blended and
contrasted with rich colours, with purples and golds, and with
greens and blues.

The sumptuous fleshy painting of the Winchester School
continues, with little development, into the eleventh century.
There is perhaps a little more economy in such manuscripts as
the missal of Robert of Jumièges (dated 1013-17) and the
Grimbald Gospels, but the overriding tradition of Winchester
ornament is patent, even in the post-Conquest period. It is
worth noting that, throughout the whole period, the decorative
initials form an important element in the manuscripts.

But there is another major tradition which is to be seen in the
Anglo-Saxon manuscripts of the tenth and eleventh centuries –
a tradition based on the art of the French school of Rheims.
One ninth-century manuscript, the Utrecht Psalter (written at
Hautevillers, near Rheims), is of particular importance in the
history of later Anglo-Saxon drawing. That it is difficult to
underestimate the importance of this style in tenth- and
eleventh-century English art is demonstrated by the copy of the
Utrecht Psalter in the British Museum, which was made in
southern England (probably at St Augustine's, Canterbury)
about 1000, and which reproduces all the breathless activity of
the original. The style of drawing is impressionistic; the figures
tend to be spindly and their protruding eyes, hunched backs
and twisted forms, together with the swirling draperies, are
executed with simple quick strokes of the pen. There is perhaps
a more linear quality about the copy than is to be found in the
original, but there is the same sense of movement and light.
This style was not intended to be used in the lush manuscripts
of the Winchester School, but its effect is felt there, as can
perhaps be seen in the New Minster Charter. It is more easily
seen in the series of scientific books of which a fairly large
number have survived. Towards the end of the eleventh

Plate 71

century the style, though still influencing English drawing, becomes more angular, while the quickly-drawn figures, with their flickering quality, are reduced to more stylized, though successful forms.

Anglo-Saxon manuscript art of this late period, then, was influenced by two Continental traditions. The first was the formalized Carolingian art, which developed into the masterly, luxurious, individual style of Winchester, and the second, the light, airy, impressionistic style of the school of Rheims, typified by the Utrecht Psalter.

SCULPTURE FROM ALFRED TO THE CONQUEST

The sculpture of the period falls into two distinct groups, that which follows the Winchester traditions and that which develops in Northumbria, based on the old vine-scroll and interlace patterns and on new Viking taste. Examples of the former are rare, while examples of the latter, although numerous often seem to be, in the words of Kendrick, 'a vast and dreary assemblage of carvings that are of indifferent quality or down-right bad.'

In the south-west of England about twenty fragments of stone sculpture, influenced by the Winchester Style, survive. The angels in the small church at Bradford-on-Avon, the 'Harrowing of Hell' scene in Bristol Cathedral and the Inglesham Crucifixion are the most famous. The draperies of these carvings are even stiffer than those of the contemporary manuscripts, while their portraiture, where it can be seen beneath the weathering, is coarse and stereotyped. The sculp-tures, however, are not without distinction, as technically they are well executed. The angel from the rood in the church of St Lawrence at Bradford-on-Avon, for example, is a very competent rendering in stone of the similar motif in the New Minster Charter, with which it must be more or less con-temporary. But none of this sculpture is really brilliant. The

Plate 73

Plate 70

Plate 75

nearest thing to brilliancy is achieved in ivory carvings, as, for example, on a triangular ivory plaque from Winchester which has much of the quality of the linear Winchester manuscripts converted into the round.

In the north of England the sculptures continue the tradition of the memorial and preaching crosses of the earlier period. The new Viking taste is reflected in the subjects which appear on them. At Halton in Lancashire, for instance, parts of the Scandinavian Sigurd Saga are represented. It was this Viking taste which helped the Northumbrians to build up a sculp-tural style which only achieved success when it was exported to Denmark – where it is known to archaeologists as the Jellinge Style. That the crude designs on the multitude of stones from the North could have blossomed into anything as accomplished as the Danish Jellinge Style seems incredible. The Vikings brought back to Northumbria a taste for animal ornament – the animals that were produced were grotesque and ugly in the extreme and it is only on metalwork that any competence is achieved. The cross from Middleton, Yorkshire, for example, bears an animal that lacks any charm but that of extreme naïvety. As with all these later Northern crosses, the technique is strictly two-dimensional: there is never any attempt to carve in the round or to give any impression of depth.

The sculpture of Mercia and eastern England shows a con-tinuation of the same dull carving that occurs in the North – interesting developments are the round-shafted crosses of Mercia (found in an area centred on Macclesfield) and the three-dimensional, house-shaped or hog's-back-shaped tomb-stones of the north-east. But the carving on most of these is undistinguished, although in many respects they have attained a grace of form which is lacking elsewhere. The Northum-brian styles even had an effect in the South; one of the crosses from Ramsbury, Wiltshire, for example, and a cross from All Hallows' Church, London, demonstrate that certain sculptors

Fig. 37. Animal ornament on a cross shaft from Middle-ton, Yorkshire

were working in a style akin to that used in the north of England.

However, one exciting monumental style did develop in England as a result of the mingling of Viking and English art, a style which is best illustrated by the vivacious tombstone from the churchyard of St Paul's Cathedral, London. Here we have a great animal carved in low relief, in a modification of the Viking Ringerike Style, charging across the stone with its head turned backwards in a flurry of zoomorphic tendril scrolls: the whole was painted and the body of the animal covered in small dots (successor perhaps of the speckled animal of the ninth century). Its great claw-like feet, its small head, its spiral hips and the long tendril with the tiny curled end are typical of an English application of a Viking art which influenced English sculpture and metalwork and even made itself felt in a small number of manuscripts. The stone dates from the early years of the eleventh century, presumably from the period when England was part of the Danish Empire. This style is the only brilliant form of barbaric sculpture that occurs in this country between the death of Alfred and the Conquest; it has a life and vitality of its own which at its best – on the St Paul's slab – is breath-taking.

Plate 74

Very little minor sculpture in this style has survived; perhaps the most accomplished is an incomplete bone plaque from the Thames which bears the representation of a man in a contorted position. The plaque is executed in the English version of the Viking Jellinge Style which, with its related Ringerike Style, was reintroduced into England in the late tenth century. In the English version of the Ringerike Style, that is, in the style of the St Paul's churchyard stone, is an ivory comb in the British Museum. On one side of this comb is a carving of an interlaced animal in the Ringerike Style, with two cat-like animals on the reverse side, whose heads are paralleled in both manuscripts and metal objects of the same period.

Plates 76, 77

THE ART OF THE METALWORKER: 900–1066

It is fitting that we should end this chapter, as we began it, with the art of the metalworker, for even at this late period metal was one of the materials the Anglo-Saxon artist could best handle. Unfortunately the richest pieces of metalwork made in this period do not survive, and we have only a series of minor objects which reflect, rather than illustrate, the glory of English metalwork. The great gold and silver figures that appear in the inventories have been melted down and all that survives are a handful of brooches and knick-knacks, and a few crude pieces of church plate. Even the richest piece of all, the gold and silver brooch from the King's School, Canterbury, is of second-rate workmanship, with clumsy degenerate animal ornament carried out in the tradition of the Trewhiddle animals in silver against a niello background. The same niello background also occurs on a pair of shrine plates, in the British Museum, bearing crudely executed animals which, while reflecting the form of the Trewhiddle animals, demonstrate the artist's struggle with the new Viking styles of Ringerike and Jellinge. The Anglo-Saxon metalworker's mastery of the Ringerike Style can be seen again in a rather crude form on a brooch from Sutton, Isle of Ely, found in the late seventeenth century with a hoard of coins of William the Conqueror. The animal and snake patterns in the four central fields of this object are quite skilful adaptations, by a second-rate craftsman, of a Viking style, tempered with the grotesque element so beloved of English artists through the ages.

The Winchester Style also appears in the metalwork, and

Fig. 38. Animal ornament on a tenth-century Anglo-Saxon shrine plate in the British Museum

Plate 78

particularly in a small group of bronzes which bear all the ornamental elements of the manuscripts, including foliage and grotesque animals. This can be seen on the censer cover from Plate 79 Canterbury, with its addorsed birds in openwork, standing on acanthus leaves in the true manner of the Winchester Style. The figural style of the Winchester manuscripts is also to be seen in metal on such pieces as the portable altar, now in the Cluny Museum, which has been described elsewhere (p. 64). Plate 16

This book, which has attempted to sketch the story of Anglo-Saxon England as seen through the eyes of the archae-ologist, finishes with a discussion of Anglo-Saxon art. English art is often underestimated, even by Englishmen. During the centuries between the fall of Rome and the coming of the Normans, English art achieved greatness on a number of occasions and the art historian can point to features of modern English art which betray distinct characteristics of Anglo-Saxon art.

It is not only the art of the Anglo-Saxons, however, which influences us today; much of modern English life stems directly from Anglo-Saxon roots. Our administrative machinery (both local and national), our laws, our parliament, our language and our literature are ultimately Anglo-Saxon in origin. They have changed through the centuries to such an extent that the Anglo-Saxon of Alfred's reign would barely recognize them, but their origins are clear enough to the historian. More tangible reminders of the Englishman's Anglo-Saxon heritage abound – the majority of English place-names were coined in this period, as were some of our personal names; the ground-plans of many of our villages and even a few of our towns were laid down by the Anglo-Saxons. The boundaries of our parishes, the broad lines of the county system, and even the method of dating historical events from the birth of Christ, are Anglo-Saxon in origin. Viking warriors, Norman kings, French administrators, German royalty, French Protestants and Central European political refugees have all been absorbed into an English nation which remains basically Anglo-Saxon.

Select Bibliography

Much of the material used in this book is drawn from short papers published in many journals of varying degree of obscurity. It would be impossible to refer to all these papers here; I have therefore listed the principal books which I have used as sources, together with one or two of the more important papers. Such original sources as the *Anglo-Saxon Chronicle*, which were actually written during the Anglo-Saxon period, are missing from the bibliography but will be found in Miss Whitelock's volume of *English Historical Documents* (cited below). The best histories of the period are those by Collingwood and Myres (for the early period) and by Stenton (for the later period). In illustration of the last chapter of the book the reader is further referred to an excellent series of colour slides of manuscripts and jewellery, published by The Colour Centre, Farnham Royal, Slough, Bucks, which give a brilliant idea of the technical and aesthetic qualities of the art of this period.

ÅBERG, N., *The Anglo-Saxons in England*, Uppsala, 1926.

ÅBERG, N., *The Occident and the Orient in the Art of the seventh century*, Stockholm, 1943-47.

AKERMAN, J. Y., *Remains of Pagan Saxondom*, London, 1855.

ALMGREN, B., *Bronsnycklar och Djurornamentik*, Uppsala, 1955 (for summary in English see: D. M. WILSON, 'Almgren and Chronology', *Medieval Archaeology*, III, 1959).

ARBMAN, H., *Svear i Österviking*, Stockholm, 1955.

BALDWIN-BROWN, G., *The Arts in Early England*, 6 vol., 1903-37.

BATTISCOMBE, C. F., (ed), *The Relics of Saint Cuthbert*, Oxford, 1956.

BAYE, J. DE, *The Industrial Arts of the Anglo-Saxons*, London, 1893.

BEHMER, E., *Das Zweischneidige Schwert der Germanischen Völker-wanderungszeit*, Stockholm, 1939.

BLAIR, P. H., *An Introduction to Anglo-Saxon England*, Cambridge, 1956.

BONSER, W., *An Anglo-Saxon and Celtic Bibliography*, Oxford, 1957.

British Museum, *Guide to Anglo-Saxon and Foreign Teutonic Antiquities*, London, 1923.

British Museum, *The Sutton Hoo Ship Burial*, 5th impression, London, 1956.

BRØGGER, A. W. AND SHETELIG, H., *The Viking Ships*, Oslo, 1951.

BRØNDSTED, J., *Early English Ornament*, London–Copenhagen, 1924.

BRUCE-MITFORD, R. L. S., 'The Sutton Hoo Ship Burial, recent theories and some comments on general interpretation', *Proc. Suffolk Institute of Archaeology and Natural History*, XXV, 1949.

CAMPBELL, A., *The Battle of Brunanburh*, London, 1938.

CHADWICK, H. M., *The Origin of the English Nation*, Cambridge, 1907.

CHADWICK, H. M., *Studies on Anglo-Saxon Institutions*, Cambridge, 1935.

CLAPHAM, A. W., *English Romanesque Architecture before the Conquest*, Oxford, 1930.

CLAPHAM, J. H. AND POWER, E. *et al.*, *The Cambridge Economic History of Europe*, Cambridge, 1941–52.

CLARK, J. G. D., *Prehistoric Europe, the Economic Basis*, London, 1952.

COLLINGWOOD, R. G. AND MYRES, J. N. L., *Roman Britain and the English Settlements*, Oxford, 1936.

CURWEN, E. C., *Plough and Pasture*, London, 1946.

DUCKETT, E. S., *St. Dunstan of Canterbury,* London, 1955.

DUCKETT, E. S., *Alfred the Great,* London, 1957.

FALK, H., *Altnordische Waffenkunde,* Kristiania, 1914.

FAUSSETT, B., *Inventorium Sepulchrale,* London, 1856.

GLOB, P., *Ard og Plov,* Aarhus, 1951.

GORDON, E. V., *The Battle of Maldon,* London, 1937.

GRABAR, A. AND NORDENFALK, C., *Early Medieval Painting,* Lausanne, 1957.

HARDEN, D. B., *(ed), Dark Age Britain,* London, 1956.

HASELOFF, G., *Der Tassilokelch,* Munich, 1951.

HILLIER, G., *The History and Antiquities of the Isle of Wight,* London, *n.d.*

HODGKIN, R. H., *A History of the Anglo-Saxons,* 2 vol. (*3rd ed.*), Oxford, 1952.

HOLMQVIST, W., *Kunstprobleme der Merowingerzeit,* Stockholm, 1939.

HOLMQVIST, W., *Germanic Art,* Stockholm, 1955.

HOSKINS, W. G., *The Making of the English Landscape,* London, 1955.

JESSEN, K. AND HELBAEK, H., *Cereals in Great Britain and Ireland in Prehistoric and Early Historic Times,* Copenhagen, 1944.

JESSUP, R. F., *Anglo-Saxon Jewellery,* London, 1950.

JOLIFFE, J. E. A., *The Jutes,* Oxford, 1933.

KELLER, M. L., *The Anglo-Saxon Weapon Names*, Heidelberg, 1906 (*Anglistische Forschungen, 15*).

KENDRICK, T. D., *Anglo-Saxon Art to 900*, London, 1938.

KENDRICK, T. D., *Late Saxon and Viking Art*, London, 1949.

KIRK, J., *The Alfred and Minster Lovell Jewels*, Oxford, 1948

KITZINGER, E., *Early Medieval Art in the British Museum* (*2nd ed.*), London, 1955.

LANE-POOLE, A., *Medieval England*, Oxford, 1958.

LEEDS, E. T., *Early Anglo-Saxon Art and Archaeology*, Oxford, 1936.

LOWE, E. A., *Codices Latini Antiquiores*, vol. II, Oxford, 1935

OMAN, C., *A History of the Art of War in the Middle Ages* (*2nd ed.*), London, 1924.

PAOR, M. AND L. DE, *Early Christian Ireland*, London, 1958.

PETERSEN, J., *De Norske Vikingesverd*, Kristiania, 1919.

PETERSEN, J., *Vikingetidens Redskaper*, Oslo, 1951.

PFEILSTÜCKER, S., '. . . *Frühangelsächsischen Kunst*', Berlin, 1936.

RICKERT, M., *Painting in Britain, The Middle Ages*, London, 1954

ROBERTSON, A. J., *Anglo-Saxon Charters* (*2nd ed.*), Cambridge, 1956

SALIN, B., *Die Altgermanische Thierornamentik* (*2nd ed.*), Stockholm, 1935.

SINGER, C., HOLMYARD, E. J., HALL, A. R. AND WILLIAMS, T. I., *A History of Technology*, vol. II, Oxford, 1956.

STEENSBERG, A., *Ancient Harvesting Implements*, Copenhagen, 1943.

STENTON, F. M., *Anglo-Saxon England*, Oxford, 1943.

STENTON, F. M., *The Bayeux Tapestry*, London, 1957.

STONE, L., *Sculpture in Britain, the Middle Ages*, London, 1955.

TALBOT RICE, D., *English Art 871–1100*, Oxford, 1952.

THOMPSON, J. D. A., *Inventory of British Coin Hoards*, London, 1956.

TISCHLER, F., 'Der Stand der Sachsenforschung, archäologisch gesehen', *Bericht der Römisch-Germanischen Kommission*, 35, 1954.

WHEELER, R. E. M., *London and the Vikings*, London, 1927.

WHEELER, R. E. M., *London and the Saxons*, London, 1935.

WHITELOCK, D., *The Beginnings of English Society*, London, 1952.

WHITELOCK, D., *English Historical Documents* London, 1955.

WORMALD, F., *English Drawings of the Tenth and Eleventh Centuries* London, 1952.

WYLIE, W., *Fairford Graves*, Oxford, 1852.

ZIMMERMANN, E. H., *Vorkarolingische Miniaturen*, Berlin, 1916.

Sources of Illustrations

The line illustrations, with the exception of Fig. 7, which is taken from Stephens', *Runic Monuments*, are either original drawings, or re-drawn from published illustrations, by Mrs Eva Wilson.

The majority of the photographs, from which the plates are made, were taken by Mr G. Ashburner of the Colour Centre. Other sources are as follows: Bibliothèque Nationale, Paris, Pl. 50; British Museum, Pl. 1, 2, 17, 18, 26, 27, 36, 37, 39, 45, 49, 52, 63, 69, 70, 79; Cambridge University Museum of Archaeology and Ethnology, Pl. 34; Mr W. Dotesio, Pl. 73; Guildhall Museum, London, Pl. 74; Mrs G. Keiller, Pl. 30, 31, 32, 43; Sir Thomas Kendrick, Pl. 22, 71; The Laurentian Library, Florence, Pl. 47; M Paul Lemare, Pl. 16; Lensmen, Dublin, Pl. 46; National Buildings Record, Pl. 13; Österreichische Licht-bildstelle, Pl. 61; Mr E. Smith, Pl. 12, 15; Dr F. Stoedtner, Pl. 48; Mr W. F. Taylor, Pl. 66; Victoria and Albert Museum, London, Pl. 51; Warburg Institute, Pl. 53, 75; and the author, Pl. 14, 25, 67, 72, 76, 77.

THE PLATES

1

2

3

4

5

6

7

8

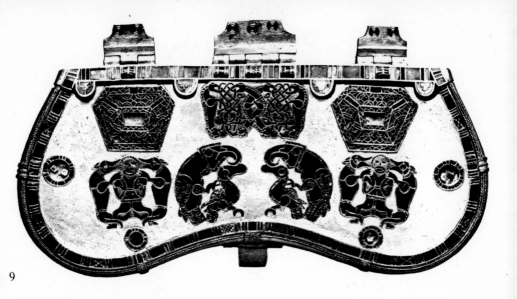

9

10

11

14

15

16

17

18

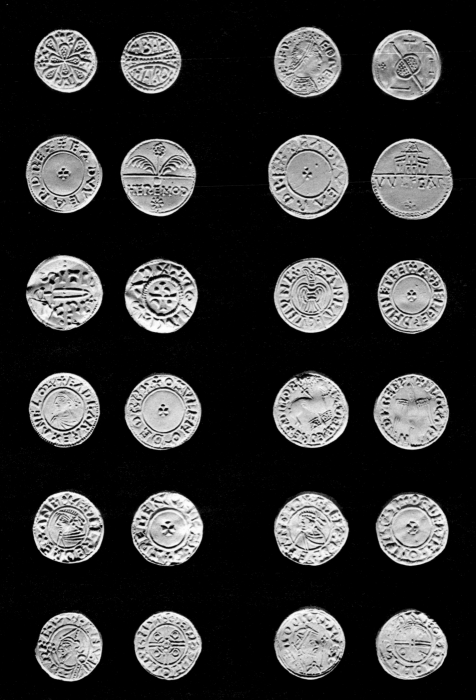

20

21

22

23

24　　　25

26

27

28

29

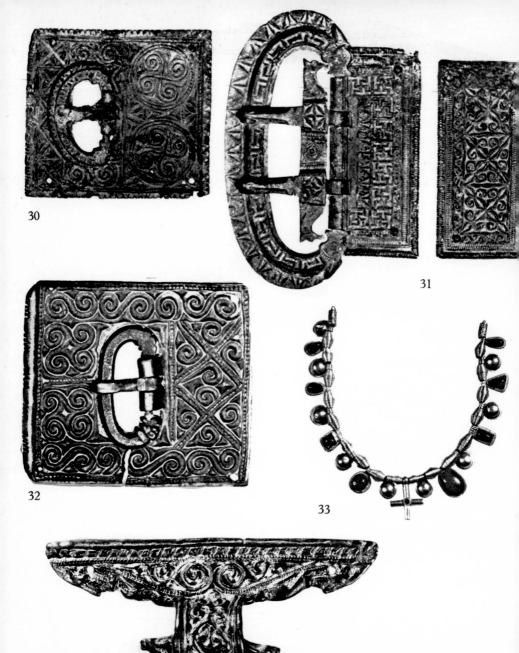

30

31

32

33

34

35

36   37   38

39

40

41

42

43

44

45

47

48

imago hominis

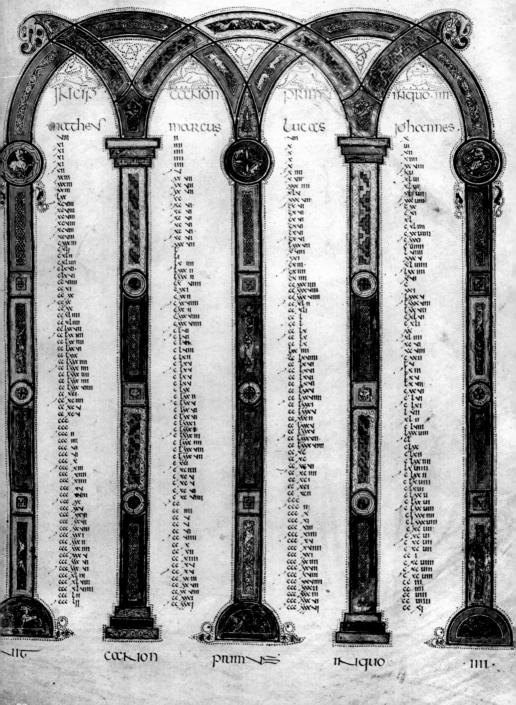

52

54

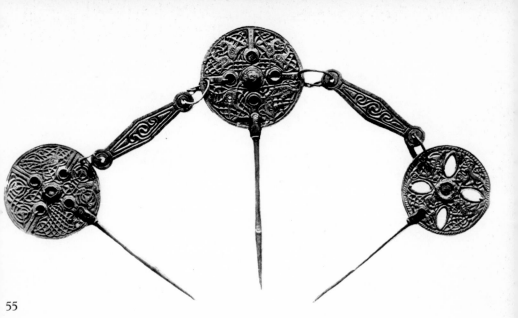

55

56

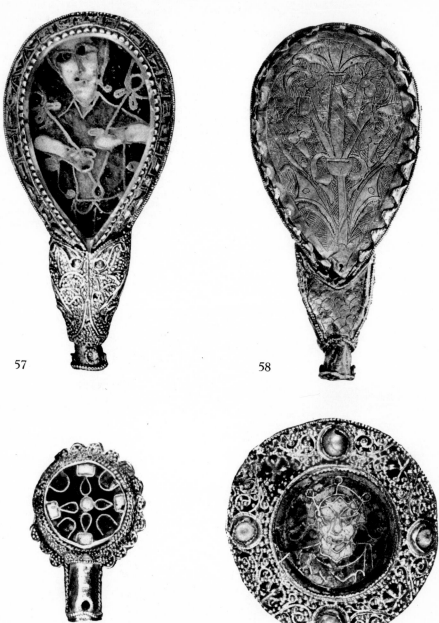

57

58

59

60

61

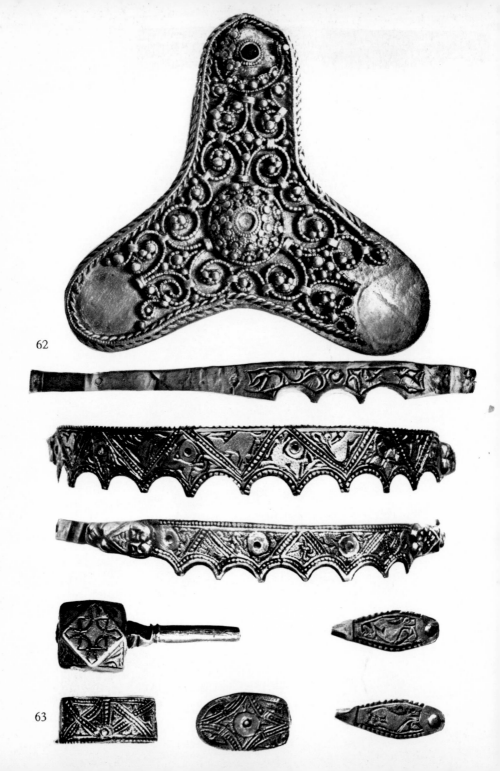

62

63

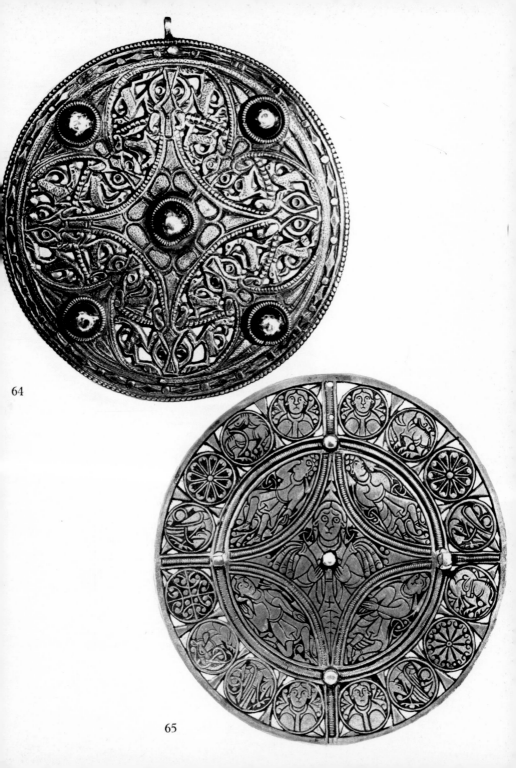

64

65

66

67

NuTIUS EceLOHICRAI PREDICANUOEL FEVAI
ECCEDNIPARILS HO NISFORSIMIL NENIWHOIS

SCA MARIA

71

72

73

74

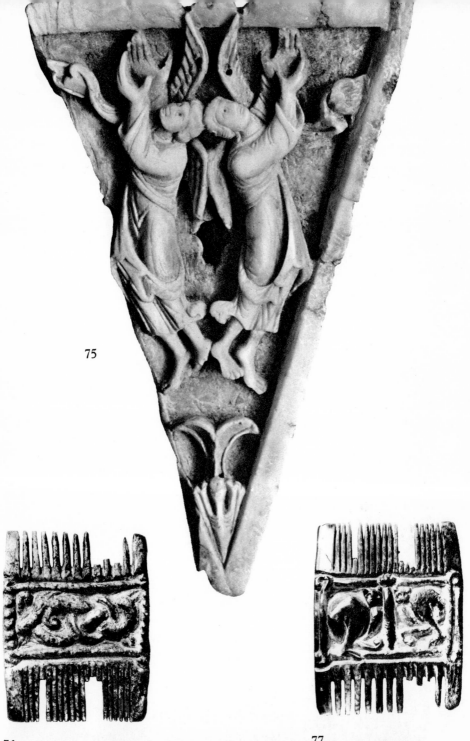

75

76   77

78

79

Notes on the Plates

In the light of the remarks in the introduction, it should be emphasized that the dates given in these notes are intended only as a general indication for the convenience of the reader.

1 One of a pair of curved jewelled clasps from the Sutton Hoo ship burial. A pin with an animal-head top, attached by a chain to the clasp, can be withdrawn to break the clasp into two parts. The clasp was sewn on to a cloth base by means of loops on the underside. The surface is decorated with garnets and mosaic glass (cf. fig. 3). Early seventh century. Length: 4·9 in. London, British Museum.

2 Gold mounts, some inlaid with garnets, from the hilt of the sword from the Sutton Hoo ship burial. The two domed circular mounts were attached to the scabbard and the truncated pyramidal mounts came, presumably, from the sword belt. Late sixth or early seventh century. Length of the pommel: 2·6 in. London, British Museum.

3 Two of a suite of ten shallow silver bowls, of provincial Byzantine origin. from the Sutton Hoo ship burial. Late sixth or early seventh century, Diameter of each: approx. 8 in. London, British Museum.

4 Small jewelled buckle from the Sutton Hoo ship burial: of gold, it is inlaid with garnets. Late sixth or early seventh century. Length: 1·8 in. London, British Museum.

5 Gold strap distributor, set with garnets, from the Sutton Hoo ship burial. The upper portion swivels laterally through 90° from the position shown in the photograph. The central element is hinged. Straps were attached by the gold rivets at the terminals. Late sixth or early seventh century. Length: 2·1 in. London, British Museum.

6 Gold buckle, decorated with garnets, from the Sutton Hoo ship burial. This buckle belongs to the same suite of mounts as the adjacent strap

distributor. Late sixth or early seventh century. Length: 3 in. London, British Museum.

7   The great buckle from the Sutton Hoo ship burial, decorated with nielloed, interlaced snakes and other animal ornament (see fig. 32). First half of the seventh century. Length: 5·2 in. London, British Museum.

8   Helmet from the Sutton Hoo ship burial. The helmet, which was probably made in Sweden in the early sixth century, consists of an iron cap covered with impressed bronze sheets and further embellished with silver and bronze gilt additions. Notice the garnets on the eyebrows. The helmet has been much restored. Height: approx. 12·5 in. London, British Museum.

9   Jewelled purse lid from the Sutton Hoo ship burial. The white background is modern; the plaques would originally have been set in leather or ivory. The cells contain garnets and fragments of mosaic glass. The purse contained 37 gold coins of Merovingian France, 3 blank coins and two ingots. Early seventh century. Length: 7·4 in. London, British Museum.

10   Terminal of the large whetstone (sceptre?) from the Sutton Hoo ship burial. The bronze cage is surmounted by a saucer-shaped plate and covers a red-painted terminal knob. Late sixth or early seventh century. Length of portion illustrated: approx. 5 in. London, British Museum.

11   Escutcheon from the inside of the largest hanging-bowl from the Sutton Hoo ship burial, showing a bronze fish standing on a pillar erected in the centre of the enamelled disc. Late sixth or early seventh century. Length of the fish: 3·6 in. London, British Museum.

12   The tower of the parish church at Earls Barton, Northamptonshire. It is the finest surviving piece of Anglo-Saxon architecture in this country. The topmost courses and the battlements of the tower are modern, but the greater portion of the tower is original Anglo-Saxon workmanship of tenth century date. The basic rubble work is plastered and enriched by pilaster strips, arcading and other sculptural details. Height of tower with modern additions: nearly 70 ft.

13 Internal view of the church at Escomb, Co. Durham (cf. also, plan on p. 58, fig. 6). The round-headed, narrow chancel arch, with its radial voussoirs, is to be noted, as are the round-headed windows and square-topped door. It may be dated to the late seventh century. Internal width of the nave: approx. 14½ ft.

14 The tenth-century apse of the parish church of All Saints at Wing, Buckinghamshire. The majority of the fabric of the Anglo-Saxon church survives, but the south aisle and tower of the church, seen in this illustration, are of fourteenth and fifteenth century date respectively. External length of the apse: 23 ft.

15 The church of St Lawrence at Bradford-on-Avon, Wiltshire. Built by Aldhelm in the late seventh or early eighth century, restored with additions in the tenth century (when the angel illustrated in pl. 73 was added) and, having been used for domestic purposes, it was rediscovered in 1858 and carefully restored. External length: approx. 48 ft.

16 Oak portable altar with porphyry centre and a parcel-gilt silver binding. At the top is a crucifixion, at the bottom an *Agnus Dei*. Also portrayed are the evangelist symbols, archangels, Mary and St John. Tenth century. Length: 10·3 in. Paris, Musée de Cluny.

17 Silver chalice from the Trewhiddle hoard (see pl. 63). One of two surviving Anglo-Saxon chalices; the inside was originally gilded. The chalice has been reconstructed. Ninth century. Height: 4·8 in. London, British Museum.

18 Two plates from a tenth-century house-shaped shrine. They are of silver, inlaid with niello, the upper plate being decorated with animal ornament (see fig. 38). Length of rectangular mount: 4·9 in. London, British Museum.

19 A selection of Anglo-Saxon silver pennies of various periods; both the obverse and the reverse of each coin are shown. Left to right: Offa, c. 785; Alfred, c. 886; Edward the Elder, c. 920; Edward the Elder,

c. 920; Sihtric the One-Eyed, c. 923; Anlaf Guthfrithson, c. 940; Edward the Martyr, c. 975; Ethelred II, summer of 1009; Ethelred II, c. 1010; Ethelred II, c. 1010; Cnut, c. 1025; Edward the Confessor, autumn of 1065. London, British Museum.

20 Group of cruciform brooches. Left to right: Greenbank, Co. Durham; West Stow Heath, Suffolk; Barrington, Cambridgeshire; Barrington, Cambridgeshire. Sixth century. Length of largest example: 5·9 in. Oxford, Ashmolean Museum.

21 Group of saucer brooches. Left to right: Cassington, Oxfordshire; Wheatley, Oxfordshire; Brighthampton, Oxfordshire; Fairford, Gloucestershire; Brighthampton; Fairford. Diameter of largest example: 3·2 in. Oxford, Ashmolean Museum.

22 The Abingdon sword. The hilt of this sword, as illustrated, has nielloed silver plates inlaid into the pommel and the guard. From New Cut Mill, Abingdon, Berkshire. Length of guard: 4·7 in. Ninth century. Oxford, Ashmolean Museum.

23 Hilt of a sword found in the bank of the River Witham, near Lincoln. The silver plates, with which it is decorated, are engraved with degenerate animal ornament and inlaid with niello. Ninth century. Length of pommel: 2·7 in. Sheffield, City Museum.

24 The Fetter Lane sword pommel. Found in Fetter Lane, London, it is executed in carved parcel-gilt silver, inlaid with niello. The design depicts a series of whirling snakes. Ninth century. Length: 3·8 in. London, British Museum.

25 Fragment of the leather scabbard of a *scramasax* from Hexham, Northumberland, decorated with an interlaced ribbon pattern. Length: 4·4 in. London, British Museum.

26 *Scramasax* found at Sittingbourne, Kent. Inlaid with copper, silver, niello and bronze, it records the name of the maker, BIORTHELM, and the owner, SIGEBEREHT. Tenth century. Length: 12·7 in. London, British Museum.

27   *Scramasax* with silver pommel and guard; found with the hanging-bowl, illustrated in pl. 45, and a spearhead in a grave at Winchester. Seventh century. Length: 15·9 in. London, British Museum.

28   The boar from the Benty Grange helmet, depicted in pl. 29. Length: 3·75 in. Sheffield, City Museum.

29   The framework of the seventh-century helmet found at Benty Grange, Derbyshire. The cap was originally made up of horn plates attached by means of the iron bands which are all that survive. The nose-piece, bottom left, bears an inlaid silver cross. Sheffield, City Museum.

30   Bronze buckle from Worms, Germany, showing the common provincial Roman chip-carved ornament. Fourth–fifth century. Length: 2·8 in. London, British Museum.

31   Bronze chip-carved buckle and counter-plate of provincial type from Kent (?). Fourth–fifth century. Length: 4·5 in. London, British Museum.

32   Bronze chip-carved buckle of provincial Roman type from Smithfield, London. Fourth–fifth century. Length: 3·2 in. London, British Museum.

33   Gold and garnet necklace from a woman's grave at Desborough, Northamptonshire. Seventh century. Length of central cross: 1 in. London, British Museum.

34   Silver-gilt, chip-carved, equal-armed brooch from Haslingfield, Cambridgeshire. The brooch might have been made on the Continent or by one of the earliest Anglo-Saxon settlers in this country. Fifth century. Length: 3·9 in. Cambridge, University Museum of Archaeology and Ethnology.

35   The Kingston Brooch. The richest piece of Anglo-Saxon jewellery found outside the Sutton Hoo grave, from Kingston Down, grave 205,

Kent. The surface is decorated with gold filigree ornament, cuttle-fish shell, garnets and lapis lazuli. The pressed foil backing to the garnets can be clearly seen in the empty cells. Seventh century. Diameter: 3·3 in. Liverpool, City Museum.

36 Jewelled disc brooch of Kentish type from Breach Down, Kent. The brooch is of silver-gilt and the zig-zag border pattern is inlaid with niello. Cast cells are inlaid with garnets. Sixth century. Diameter: 1·5 in. London, British Museum.

37 Jewelled disc brooch of Kentish type from Faversham, Kent. Sixth century. Diameter: 1·6 in. London, British Museum.

38 Gold and garnet pendant from Faversham, Kent. The flat back-plate is decorated with filigree wire, the three whirling animal-heads in the centre being executed in cloisonné garnets. The eyes of the animals are set *en cabochon*. Seventh century. Diameter: 4·5 in. London, British Museum.

39 Gold and garnet buckle plate, from Wynaldum, Friesland, Holland, built up on a silver back-plate. In the upper panel are a pair of tortuous backward-looking quadrupeds. Seventh century. Length: 3·7 in. Leeuwarden (Holland), Fries Museum.

40 Pectoral cross of St Cuthbert. This cross was found in the tomb of St Cuthbert in Durham Cathedral. It was presumably placed in the coffin on the death of St Cuthbert in 687. The lower arm has been damaged and repaired in antiquity. Of gold, shell and garnet, it is one of the latest pieces of garnet jewellery known from an Anglo-Saxon context. Seventh century. Breadth: 2·35 in. Durham, Cathedral Library.

41 The Ixworth cross. Found in a grave at Stanton, Ixworth, Suffolk, it is of gold inlaid with thick garnets. Seventh century. Breadth: 1·5 in. Oxford, Ashmolean Museum.

42 The Wilton cross. This gold and garnet jewelled pendant, found at Wilton, Norfolk, contains a coin of Heraclius (610–41), the Byzantine

Emperor. Perhaps from the Sutton Hoo workshop. Seventh century. Height: 1·9 in. London, British Museum.

43 Enamelled bronze mounts from a hanging-bowl found at Middleton by Youlgrave, Derbyshire. Sixth—seventh century. Diameter of disc: 2·1 in. Sheffield, City Museum.

44 Two gold clasps, ornamented with filigree techniques, and a gold and garnet buckle, from a rich seventh-century barrow at Taplow, Buckinghamshire. Length of buckle: 4 in. London, British Museum.

45 Hanging-bowl, found, with a spearhead and the *scramasax* illustrated in pl. 27, in a grave at Winchester. The escutcheon is inlaid with red enamel. Seventh century. Diameter at rim: 11·1 in. London, British Museum.

46 The Book of Durrow (fol. 21b). Portrait of the Evangelist Matthew. The body of the Evangelist is an abstract expression of the naturalism of the Mediterranean model from which it is derived. The colours of the page are red, yellow and green. Second half of the seventh century. Length of page: 9·6 in. Dublin, Library of Trinity College.

47 Codex Amiatinus. This page (the Ezra folio) has in the past been described as Italian. Recent research, however, suggests most strongly that it is Anglo-Saxon and it illustrates well the classicism of a certain type of seventh-century Anglo-Saxon manuscript art. Length of page: 19·4 in. Florence, Biblioteca Laurentiana.

48 The Lindisfarne Gospels (fol. 47b). One of the great carpet pages, illuminated with interlaced animals and birds. Painted just before the year 700. Length: 13·5 in. London, British Museum.

49 The Lindisfarne Gospels (fol. 25b). Page portraying the Evangelist John, surmounted by his symbol, Painted just before the year 700. Length: 13·5 in. London, British Museum.

50 Echternach Gospels (fol. 18b). Symbol of the Evangelist Matthew,

painted in Northumbria (possibly in the Lindisfarne *scriptorium*) about the year 700. Length: 10·3 in. Paris, Bibliothèque Nationale.

51 St Chad Gospels (p. 142). Portrait of the Evangelist Mark, surmounted by his symbol the lion. Painted in Northumbria in the early eighth century. Length: 9·7 in. Lichfield, Cathedral Library.

52 Page of cannon tables from the MS Royal 1.E.VI (fol. 4a) in the British Museum. In the borders, which surround these tables of concordance, are ornaments which can be compared to that on eighth- and ninth-century metalwork. Early ninth century. Length: 18·5 in. London, British Museum.

53 The Ruthwell Cross. Two views, showing on one face various Christian scenes and on the side a typical Northumbrian inhabited vine-scroll. Ruthwell, Dumfries.

54 Panel from St Cuthbert's coffin. Upper half of the figure of Christ carved on the lid of the coffin reliquary. His right hand is raised in blessing and He carries a book in His left hand. Late seventh century. Durham, Cathedral Library.

55 The Witham pins (cf. fig. 33). Set of three, linked, circular, gilt-bronze pins found in the river Witham, near Fiskerton, Lincolnshire. The ornament is executed in the chip-carved technique and the eyes of the animals are inlaid with blue glass. Eighth century. Length of central pin: 4·7 in. London, British Museum.

56 The Franks Casket. Whalebone ivory casket, of Northumbrian workmanship, carved with scenes from a universal history. The scenes are surrounded by inscriptions in runes. Early eighth century. Length: 8·8 in. London, British Museum.

57 The Alfred Jewel. Made of gold with a cloisonné enamel portrait set under crystal. This jewel was found at Newton Park, Somerset in 1693. Round the edge of the upper portion is an inscription which, when translated, reads, *Alfred ordered me to be made.* This presumably

refers to King Alfred (871–99). Length: 2·9 in. Oxford, Ashmolean Museum.

58 Back of the Alfred Jewel, showing the engraved foliate pattern on the gold back‑plate.

59 The Minster Lovell jewel. Found at Minster Lovell, Oxfordshire. Con‑ structed in the same manner as the Alfred Jewel (pl. 57), it is perhaps slightly later in date (tenth century?). Length: 1·25 in. Oxford, Ashmolean Museum.

60 The Dowgate Hill brooch. Found in Dowgate Hill, London, it is of gold filigree and enamel. Its close resemblance to the Alfred Jewel (pl. 57) is very striking. Ninth–tenth century. Diameter: 1·3 in. London, British Museum.

61 The Tassilo Chalice. Gilt bronze vessel inscribed with the name of Tassilo III, Duke of Bavaria 748–88, and given by him to the monastery of Kremsmünster, which was founded in 777. Height: 10·5 in. Kremsmünster Monastery, Austria.

62 The Kirkoswald brooch. This filigree silver trefoil brooch, set with garnets (of which only one survives), was found at Kirkoswald, Cum‑ berland, with coins which date its deposition to between 850 and 860. Eighth–ninth century. Length: 3·5 in. London, British Museum.

63 Material from the Trewhiddle Hoard (see also pl. 17 and fig. 35). Found at Trewhiddle, near St Austell, Cornwall, with coins which date its deposition to *c.* 875. The objects shown include strap ends, strap slides, pin and curved drinking‑horn mounts. Many of the objects are decorated with animal ornament in the 'Trewhiddle style'. London, British Museum.

64 The Strickland brooch. Of silver, inlaid with gold plates and niello, it is so called after Sir William Strickland who is presumed to have acquired it in the early nineteenth century. Ninth century. Diameter: 4·3 in. London, British Museum.

65 The Fuller brooch. A silver disc brooch inlaid with niello and portraying, in the central panels, the five senses, taste, smell, hearing, touch and sight. Ninth century. Diameter: 4·4 in. London, British Museum.

66 Head of a carved stone cross from Cropthorne, Worcestershire. Ninth century.

67 Bone trial-piece from Station Road, York. Showing animals (similar in style to those on objects from the Trewhiddle hoard) being tried out on a piece of discarded bone. Ninth century. Length: 4·3 in. York, Yorkshire Museum.

68 Two portions of the stole of St Cuthbert, executed at Winchester (?) between 909 and 916 and probably presented to the shrine of St Cuthbert by King Aethelstan in 934. Left, St Peter—right, Jonah. Length of portion illustrated: approx. 7 in. Durham, Cathedral Library.

69 Page (fol. 5b) from the Benedictional of St Aethelwold, illustrating the Annunciation. This page illustrates the height of Winchester lavishness. Made for, or at the order of, Aethelwold, Bishop of Winchester 975–80. Length 11·5 in. London, British Museum.

70 Page (fol. 2b) from the Charter of the New Minster at Winchester. King Edgar is seen offering the charter to Christ, who sits in a mandorla. The page must have been painted in, or shortly after, 966. Length: 8·125 in. London, British Museum.

71 Detail of fol. 51b of a psalter (British Museum MS., Harley 603). Executed in a variety of coloured inks; the colours used in the portion illustrated (the heading of Psalm 103) are red, black, blue and brown. Date: *c.* 1000. Height of the portion illustrated: approx. 4·5 in. London, British Museum.

72 Fragments of Anglo-Saxon carved stone crosses and tombstones in the porch of Bakewell Church, Derbyshire. The fragments illustrate different styles of Anglo-Saxon interlace ornament.

73 Angel, carved in stone, from the church of St Lawrence at Bradford-on-Avon (see pl. 15). One of the finest pieces of late Saxon stone sculpture it can be compared with angels depicted in pl. 70 and 75. Tenth century. Length: about 5 ft.

74 Tombstone from St Paul's churchyard, London, executed in the Ringerike Style. The surface was originally painted with two or three colours and the body of the animal was speckled with white dots. Tenth–eleventh century. Length: 2 ft. London, the Guildhall Museum.

75 Ivory panel, from Winchester, carved in the Winchester Style: an expression in ivory of the figural style which can be seen in pl. 70 and 73. Tenth century. Height approx. 3 in. Winchester, City Museum.

76– Two sides of a comb of walrus ivory, showing on one face an interlaced
77 animal inspired by Viking art and on the other an Anglo-Saxon animal which can be compared with those on the censer cover illustrated in pl. 79. Tenth century. Height 2·1 in. London, British Museum.

78 The Sutton brooch. Found at Sutton, Isle of Ely, in 1694 with coins of William I. The brooch is decorated with Ringerike Style ornament. On the back of the brooch is inscribed a curse in Anglo-Saxon. Tenth–eleventh century. Diameter: 5·9 in. London, British Museum.

79 Bronze censer-cover, from Canterbury, in the form of a building: the lower borders and the hips of the animals are inlaid with nielloed silver plates. Tenth–eleventh century. Height: 4·7 in. London, British Museum.

Index